Margaret E. Baird

TELEVISION BAIRD

TELEVISION BAIRD

MARGARET BAIRD

HAUM

CAPE TOWN · PRETORIA

1973

ISBN 0 7986 0052 7

First published by HAUM, 58 Long Street, Cape Town
Printed by Citadel Press, Lansdowne, Cape

for Diana and Malcolm

Contents

I.	*The making of a genius*	13
II.	*Undersocks, romance and jam*	28
III.	*Soap, more romance and television*	36
IV.	*Electrocution and bribery*	46
V.	*Flicker and detail*	58
VI.	*Across the Atlantic*	73
VII.	*"How strange is the world"*	82
VIII.	*In some way different*	94
IX.	*"But the horses could be seen"*	102
X.	*The rival*	115
XI.	*The fighter*	131
XII.	*War and other irritations*	143
XIII.	*Keeping right on*	152

Illustrations

John Logie Baird as portrayed by the artist Anatas Botzaritch Sava frontispiece

A photograph of John Logie Baird taken by himself as a boy 32

Baird in Glasgow, 1915 33

The jam factory in Trinidad 33

The original Baird transmitter 48

An experimental scanning disc 49

The first television photograph ever taken 80

John Logie Baird and Margaret Baird 81

Baird in his laboratory 96

Baird and his son 97

Addressing a convention on television 128

Demonstrating the Telechrome 129

The Baird house in London 144

Leslie Mitchell and William Taynton 144

Baird's "firsts" 145

I wish to express my sincere thanks to Mr Eldred Green for his invaluable assistance in the writing of this book.

—Margaret Baird

I. *The making of a genius*

In the genius of John Logie Baird an important element was determination. He believed that television was possible, but it was his determination to prove that his belief was reasonable and to profit by it that made him the inventor of television. His determination could take other forms, an example being the way he decided to take a woman he loved away from her husband and then carried out his decision; but that was before he met and married me.

With determination went a rational mind, intellectual power, wide reading, and an imagination that was stimulated to action by a writer such as H. G. Wells, who was producing science fiction that was credible to John Baird when he was a boy.

Shaping the later development of his career were the facts of his birth and upbringing in Glasgow or, rather, in the neighbourhood of Glasgow, and the presence there of other boys and young men such as Jack Buchanan, who was to become an actor-manager, and John Reith, who was to become director-general of the British Broadcasting Corporation.

Jack Buchanan, a friend from childhood, was to play a part in John's career as an inventor in London. John Reith was to be in charge of broadcasting in Britain during the period that John Baird was striving to have television recognized as a service with a great future and when subsequent inventors were challenging Baird's system of television with a later system of their own.

About John Reith, very much the public-school type as a youth and young man, son of the Moderator of the United Free Church of Scotland, in contrast to John Baird, son of the minister of St Bride's church in Helensburgh and the product of rather a pretentious private school, it is best to have John Baird's own words. He wrote of an experience at the Royal

Technical College, Glasgow: "I met Reith for the first time in rather unfavourable circumstances. I was, and still am, very short-sighted, and at the beginning of one of the classes the professor asked if those who were short-sighted and wanted front seats would hand in their names. When I went up to the platform to give my name, three large and impressive students were talking to him. They talked on terms of equality; in fact there was a distinct aroma of patronage. They boomed with heavy joviality at the poor little professor who was distinctly embarrassed and ill at ease. I interrupted timidly and handed the professor a piece of paper with my name on it. As I did so the heaviest and most overpowering of those students turned round and boomed at me: 'Ha! What's the matter with you? Are you deaf or blind?' I simpered something inaudible and he turned his back on me."

The young man who turned his back on John Baird was John Charles Walsham Reith, destined to become Lord Reith, general manager of the British Broadcasting Company (1922-1927), first director-general of the British Broadcasting Corporation (1927-1938), first chairman of the British Overseas Airways Corporation, and head of other organizations not relevant in the growth of television.

After they had sat together in the same class, Baird becoming an electrical engineer and Reith a civil engineer, they were not to meet again for twenty years and in very different circumstances, but then Reith was unable to dispel the feeling of awe and dislike which he had created in Baird at their first meeting.

Glasgow provided another friend who was to influence John's life, a life as much one of friendship and love as of a concentrated pursuit of an engineering goal. This friend was Guy Fullarton Robertson, later nicknamed Mephistopheles – Mephy for short. Like Jack Buchanan, he was a friend from childhood.

Glasgow plays a complex part in the story, for it was revolt against working as an electrical engineer under bad conditions there that made John try his hand at inventing and business, teaching him that he had business ability to supplement his inventiveness. It was the two thousand pounds that he made in Glasgow from the Baird Undersock that enabled him to escape from Glasgow's climate to Trinidad and the adventure of his factory for making jam and chutney. It was London's climate and air that drove him to Hastings, but it was his friend of Glasgow days, Mephy, who made him choose Hastings.

Living in Hastings he needed money and set to work on television. Wireless was then just coming into its own for entertainment and civilian communication, and he believed that if it was possible to hear over a long distance by wireless telegraphy, it was also possible to see at a distance by wireless – wireless serving television.

But to return to the little boy whose character was taking shape. His father, the Reverend John Baird, was a jovial man in company but a stern father who, in the fashion of his time and place, preached hell-fire and damnation to his children as well as to his congregation.

John, a sensitive child and very frail after a long illness at the age of two, was the youngest of four children. At one time, when eight years old, he was so frightened that he spent an entire winter's night on his knees beside his bed, frantically praying for forgiveness.

For all that he was a happy little boy, made thrifty by his background. Pocket-money in the family was a half-penny a week. The two sisters spent theirs on sweets; John saved his half-pennies for twelve weeks until he had sixpence to buy a toy camera which he had been watching all that time in a shop window, fearful that it would be sold before he could afford to buy it.

John grew up in the Baird home called *The Lodge* and in the environment of Helensburgh. In the home was lively and educated conversation, even if it was naïve and unworldly. In Helensburgh there was abundant neighbourliness, everyone knowing everyone else, but there were many classes and divisions. After the untouchables – the tramps, gipsies, and beggars – came the dustmen, labourers, and navvies. Some distance from these were the smaller tradesmen: the butchers, bakers, and grocers. These merged into the businessmen in a small way, and the businessmen expanded into the city magnates. In this stratum, but oscillating between its extremes, were the professional men: the doctors, the lawyers, the clergy. A race apart were the country gentlemen, the county's landowners, engaged in huntin', shootin', and fishin'. Right at the top was the laird, Sir Iain Colquhoun of Luss.

This was the structure of the society in which John was reared and which had a profound formative influence on his character and outlook.

John left a record* of his early years, enabling me to describe incidents accurately, supplementing my memories of what he told me with the frank notes which he made. His style of writing is lucid. In the notes a pattern may be seen as it emerges, a pattern of awareness of scientific developments around him, a desire to apply new discoveries and inventions to his own life, and an emotional response to the poverty and misery which – as the son of a minister of the Scottish Church with a wife who did good works among the poor – he could not help but see. These elements in the pattern followed a period when religion was warping his emotional life.

John was born in 1888 when his father was already forty-seven years of age and a man of settled habits accustomed to his own way. Born in 1841, the Reverend John Baird entered Glasgow University in 1860, helping to support himself by tutoring, and graduating M.A. with honours in classics. He

*His unpublished autobiography, *Socks, Sermons and Television.*

then obtained the degree of bachelor of divinity and in 1868 was chosen to open a new church in Helensburgh.

In 1878 he married Jessie Morrison Inglis, the orphaned niece of a Glasgow ship-builder. As the church had no manse Mr Baird used his bride's dowry to buy *The Lodge*, a square house of stone, one storey high, recently built by an elderly woman whose ambition in life was to own the largest dining-room in Helensburgh. Her ambition achieved, she died.

John, junior, was the fourth child. His mother, much younger than her husband, was a sweet and pious woman. She devoted herself to her children, was prepared to make almost any sacrifice for them, especially for the younger son, John, always ailing after a serious illness at the age of two.

In addition to caring for her four children, Jessie Baird had many parochial duties as the minister's wife, and these included visiting the poor. John was away from school very often because of his delicate health, so he was taken to the homes of the poor by his mother and saw what poverty could mean.

The Reverend John Baird was a man of the period and the force in the household. As he prospered he was able to indulge what today would be called eccentricities. The family was to eat at conventional hours, but he had to have his dinner at three in the afternoon, meaning extra work for his wife, even though *The Lodge* had its servants.

He was plainly spoken to the point of rudeness, and his wealthier parishioners took him abroad on journeys to Norway and Africa, it is said for the pleasure of his pithier comments. He had studied comparative religion, and in spite of preaching hell-fire and damnation he could say to a theological student who took the story of Jonah literally: "Aye, Willie, you and the whale rival each other in swallowing capacity." And when John, junior, rebelling against his father's wish that he, too, should enter the ministry, said at the age of fourteen that he did not think he could be a sufficiently good hypocrite, the answer came: "I think you could manage that all right."

But it is worth seeing the father through the eyes of the son: "In those days any man over fifty had become a pompous, elderly figure. Those were not the days of romping papas in shorts. Papa was an impressive figure, with a large beard, still brown, through which he boomed at his children in the manner of an oracle. To me he was to be avoided as a source of embarrassment and uneasiness."

As the family grew in numbers, increased in age, and made more noise, the minister added another floor to *The Lodge* and turned this into a study. Communication between the floor below and the floor above was by speaking-tube. No child dared knock at the door of the study; instead, the child blew up the speaking-tube and a whistle stuck in the end of the tube within the study whistled to announce that someone below wished to speak with the one above.

In that study the minister received his parishioners, wrote his sermons, and married young couples, for weddings in church had not yet become the fashion.

The steepness and darkness of the staircase between the floors were to bring to an end John's experimental installation of electric light in *The Lodge*.

Sundays in the home were austere and the effect of his religious upbringing is best left to John: "Fear hung over me in my childhood like a dark cloud. It was fear not only of God but of intangible evil, of ghosts and spirits, creatures of unimaginable horror, waiting and watching for an opportunity to get at me. At night I was put to bed at eight o'clock and left to lie in abject terror. I covered myself with the blankets, leaving only a little hole for breathing, while the grey lady crept up to my bedside, or the two supernatural old men crouched at the foot of my bed, watching and waiting. A burglar or a tiger would have been a welcome intrusion.

"I went through a phase resembling the state of mind of

the children of Israel, propitiating an angry, jealous Deity. I prayed interminably and felt that sacrifices were demanded of me. I went on praying, fearing God, and making propitiatory gestures long after my reason regarded such things as altogether contemptible and ridiculous."

Accompanying his mother on visits to the poor formed John's political opinions. There were no slums in Helensburgh, for that was a place where the prosperous could escape from Glasgow. But John saw respectable people reduced to poverty, misery, and despair, until semi-starvation and privation carried them to the local poor-law institution, the workhouse, or the grave. By contrast the upper classes, in some mysterious manner, were secure from want. The contrast between the poor and the rich was etched on his mind, and to the end of his days he sometimes wore a cloth cap as a symbol of his socialist sympathies, his dislike and distrust of the wealthy.

He had a respect for the gentry, a feeling he shared with most of the middle class of Helensburgh, and because of his poor health he had a horror of personal poverty.

John and his brother went to Larchfield, a private school in Helensburgh, where they were not good at the classics, where no science was taught, where the mathematics was a farce. John was no good at games, and the cold showers after games each afternoon gave him chill after chill.

But John had a talent for making friends. Jack Buchanan, already something of a dandy, and Guy Fullarton Robertson have been mentioned; others at Larchfield were Jimmy Bonner (killed in World War I), Jack Bruce, Neil Whimster, who became a Glasgow ship-owner, and Godfrey Harris.

It was with these companions that John's real education began and the pattern of his life began to emerge.

Science was in the air and changes were coming, though information travelled slowly. For all that, scientific and engineering information was reaching John and his friends.

More to the point, scientific and engineering events were happening near by. Cardross was next to Helensburgh, and it was there that Percy Pilcher, a lecturer at Glasgow University, had flown his glider in 1898. Henry Bell, who launched the first successful steamship in Europe, had lived in Helensburgh. Alexander Graham Bell, born in Edinburgh, had patented the electric telephone in 1876. Edison had patented the incandescent electric lamp with carbon filaments in 1880, Willoughby Smith had reported the photo-conductivity effect in selenium in the *Journal of the Society of Telegraph Engineers* in 1873, George Eastman had perfected dry film in 1880. With the slow diffusion of information, especially to schoolboys who were taught no science, a few years in the nineteenth century could be the equivalent of a few weeks today.

The camera John had saved his half-pennies for was nothing but a toy, but then he was still a little boy. When he was at Larchfield he bought a Lizar's quarter-plate Perfecta, and as owner of this masterpiece he was elected president of the photographic society. The meetings he presided over were opened with formality, then articles on photography were read and photographs taken by members were passed around for criticism. But a spirit of levity intruded and after several schoolboy pranks the society ceased to exist.

The next event was an experiment in aviation. Influenced by Wilbur and Orville Wright, who had begun by flying gliders, as had Percy Pilcher, before installing an engine for powered flight in 1903, John and Godfrey Harris read everything they could on flying. Then they decided to build an aeroplane, which turned out to be a weird contraption like two box-kites joined in the centre, quite conventional for those days. After weeks of work it was ready to fly, or rather to glide, for it had no engine. They were consciously following the example of the Wright brothers by gliding before they flew with power, but they intended to fit an engine in due course.

They hoisted their flying machine on to the flat roof of the kitchen at *The Lodge* and John took his seat in it, but with no intention of flying. Godfrey Harris had other ideas and in spite of one shout of alarm from John he pushed the machine over the edge of the roof. Airborne, the machine rocked wildly in the air, broke in half, and John landed with a bump on the lawn behind the kitchen door. In spite of the force with which he hit the ground no bones were broken, but the experience of flying was enough for a lifetime and John never went up in an aeroplane.

Photography and aviation were no more than minor probings of the world of engineering. The next venture determined his eventual career: it was communication at a distance.

John was thirteen or fourteen when a book called *The Boys' Book of Stories and Pastimes* came his way. Alexander Graham Bell, who moved from Scotland to Canada in 1870, had patented the electric telephone in 1876. But before the telephone was electrically operated at greater efficiency, mechanical telephones had existed.

The book in John's hands gave instructions on how to make a simple telephone with thread and cocoa-tins and then how to make a more ambitious model with wire, nails, and pill-boxes. Telephones became a mania with John. He made a small telephone-exchange in his room with wires running over the street to the houses where lived his friends Neil Whimster, Jack Bruce, Ian Norwell, and Godfrey Harris. More plans were made but an accident brought the enterprise to an end.

In Helensburgh was a cabby known as Old MacIntyre. One windy night he was driving his cab home when he was caught around the neck by a telephone wire, dragged from his box, and thrown cursing and shouting into the gutter. Shaking in his fury he ran to the house of Mr McDonald, a mild and inoffensive man who was the manager of the National Telephone Company in Helensburgh. To McDonald Old MacIntyre shouted: "What the devil do you mean by having wires hanging over the road? I'll have the law on your company and I'll wring your bloody neck!"

It looked as if an unpleasant lawsuit would develop and John had an anxious time, for the wires had nothing to do with the National Telephone Company; they belonged to the Baird telephone system. But Old MacIntyre and the Reverend John Baird were good friends and the affair was settled quietly.

That was the end of the telephone exchange, but it did not matter, for John was busy installing electric light in *The Lodge*. As *The Helensburgh Times* put it, *The Lodge* was "enjoying the amenities of electric light, thanks to the ingenuity of a younger member of the household".

John had bought an oil engine second-hand and had made a small dynamo. His accumulators consisted of a great number of lead plates wrapped in flannelette and packed in jam jars filled with sulphuric acid. In making the accumulators he got some sort of lead poisoning which left a scar on a hand.

He lit the staircase in the house with a series of electric bulbs of low power, and the system worked well provided that the incipient electrical engineer supervised it. But his interest turned to other things, and one dark night the minister above, descending from his study to his bedroom on the ground floor, fell down the staircase because it was unlighted. In his fury he had the gas lights brought back and the dynamo was banished to a shed.

The next experiment was a primitive attempt at television, but the family noticed nothing but a bad smell on the stove in the kitchen. John was trying to make a selenium cell by wrapping a wire around a piece of porcelain, heating this device, and rubbing it with a stick of selenium. He learnt from this experiment that the current from a selenium cell is very small indeed, too small for the use he wanted to put it to.

I have not been able to establish exactly when John made

this youthful attempt at inventing television, but it was probably not later than 1903, when he was fifteen.

When, later, his fortunes were at a low ebb, he remembered this early attempt at television when he took up the subject again, in 1923. By that date an amplifier was available. In his own words: "The problem of amplifying the current from a selenium cell was solved by the united efforts of Fleming and De Forest. It was their work which supplied the missing link and made television possible. I was, indeed, the first to produce television images but without the amplifier based on Fleming's valve with De Forest's grid I would have been hopelessly stuck."

John had early rejected his father's request that he go into the ministry and it seemed obvious that he would turn to engineering, especially electrical engineering, so in 1906, at the age of eighteen, he enrolled at the Royal Technical College, Glasgow. There the professor of electrical engineering was Dr Angus Maclean, author of the great standard works on electricity and electrical engineering.

With his poor health, which did not stand up well to the slow and often cold journeys by train between Helensburgh and Glasgow, John was often absent from the Tech. and he took eight years to graduate, becoming an Associate of the Royal Technical College, Glasgow, in 1914. The subjects for his degree were mathematics, electrical engineering, and motive-power engineering. He obtained no honours.

To begin with he was keen enough, but he grew bored. In his own words: "On leaving Larchfield I went to the Royal Technical College in Glasgow, filled with zeal and enthusiasm and feeling quite sure I should distinguish myself. I found it not so easy. There were plenty of other youths there filled with zeal and determination. How these youths worked! They were, for the most part, working men, bright lads out to make a career for themselves. They were not the intellectual cream (those won scholarships and went to the university);

nevertheless they were doughty competitors. Nothing could approach the frenzied concentration with which they absorbed learning. There was no pretence at social life: there was no time for it.

"The first year I was there I learned a good deal that was very useful and interesting; the remaining years were, I think, almost entirely a waste of time. I learned, with great pains and boredom, masses of formulae and tedious dates, of which much was never used and soon forgotten. But what I learned in the first year remained with me all my life and has been of great value."

In spite of boredom and ill health John enjoyed those years. He later said in jest that he had deliberately prolonged them. The father was paying the fees, the son, with his lively mind, was pursuing a wide variety of private interests.

For five pounds John bought a motor-cycle, second hand. It had a tiny engine beneath the seat and was called a Kellycomb Antoinette. With this he roared about the countryside. He sold the motor-cycle and bought a three-wheeled motor-car, a scrapheap on wheels, known in Helensburgh as "young Baird's reaper and binder" from the noise it made. With him in the three-wheeler went his friend Godfrey Harris, then studying at the university.

John and Godfrey discussed anything and everything, metaphysics and their growing doubts about religious beliefs. With some reluctance John became an agnostic and tried out his new ideas on ministers visiting *The Lodge*. He later said of this period: "When an arrogant young man, I tried again and again to convert to agnosticism the clergy who came to our house as 'pulpit supplies'. With their references to the original Greek testament and vast verbal smokescreens they twisted and turned far into the night . . . The old clergy baffled me by repudiating reason and intelligence alike and appealing to faith."

Besides working out his own ideas he was reading widely, from Goethe, Tolstoy, Voltaire, and Shakespeare to W. W.

Jacobs and Jerome K. Jerome, but above them all was H. G. Wells, whom he regarded as a demi-god.

There were two sides to H. G. Wells, his imaginative science fiction and his accounts of the struggles of Kipps and Mr Lewisham. John was beginning to realize that his own position in the world was not far above theirs, apart from the security which his doting mother provided at *The Lodge*.

During the long vacations in those eight years he had to take various jobs, and to him this work was a horrifying revelation.

In 1909 he worked as an apprentice engineer in Halley's Industrial Motors at Yonker, his hours being from six in the morning to half-past five in the evening, though incessant overtime usually kept him at work until eight. To him the work was "soul-destroying, monotonous drudgery". He had to use a chisel and chip a little groove in each of the casings in a pile. Week after week he chipped these grooves, with all around him "the most sordid conditions". Work in the Argyle Motor Works was little better.

These experiences gave him a deep-seated grudge against the gilded youth whose photographs he saw in the fashionable magazines in dentists' waiting-rooms, for in addition to his poor health he had a lot of toothache and eventually lost most of his teeth. His bitterness against those who moved in circles which the Tech. considered exclusive extended to those whose positions were assured, whether they passed their examinations or not. Among these was John Reith.

Life at *The Lodge* had one drawback. In Helensburgh a young man with no prospects found it difficult to speak to a young woman, and a love affair was out of the question. John put up with the conventional restraints, thinking that when he went into digs all would be well. But he was not of the stuff of which Don Juans are made. Circumstances and temperament were against him.

He was shy and nervous. His unsuccessful attempts to

pick up a girl made him more frustrated. Eventually he became adroit, but more of that later.

Marriage was out of the question for a man in his position. His temperament and passions were too strong for celibacy, so an affair was the only way left open to him.

But life and a career were facing him, and with typical Baird indolence he tried to evade a decision by prolonging his education. He was twenty-six when he graduated from the Tech.

Again he tried to postpone a decision, this time by entering Glasgow University where, as an Associate of the Royal Technical College, he could graduate as a bachelor of science in six months. His father agreed, and John was very happy at the university. He enjoyed himself and did not take his degree.

A note is needed about two of John's friends who had an influence upon the shape of his life: Godfrey Harris, who had pushed the flying machine off the kitchen roof with John in it and would in the years to come lure him to Trinidad, and Guy Fullarton Robertson, nicknamed Mephy.

Godfrey Harris was in Glasgow for most of the time that John was there. He was another independent Scot who could not bear regular hours, take orders, or work to a routine, and he lacked the practical streak which John was to discover in himself. After graduating in science at the university, Harris started a business in Glasgow. The business was not a success and he packed up and left for the New World. From there he wrote to John from time to time.

The end to which Godfrey Harris came was somewhat bizarre. John wrote: "He was a mass of brain and initiative, but like Mephy and myself he had a kink. He could not stand routine work, he could not be an employee – he wanted freedom! He went off to the United States of America, where he kept a job as a draftsman until he had saved a little money. Then he threw up his job, bought a few acres of land for a paltry sum at a place called Wadsville, in the wilds of Louisiana near the hill-billies, built himself a shack, bought a few goats and hens, planted vegetables, and found himself practically self-supporting, a strange life for a bachelor of science. His only neighbours were illiterate hill-billies. Their religion, he told me, was Holy Rolling. After the church service, consisting of hymns and prayers, all the lights in the hall were put out. The congregation, both male and female, became possessed by the Holy Ghost and rolled together on the floor in a vast religious ecstasy, screaming, moaning, and clutching each other in the throes of their possession. The number of illegitimate births, he said, was unparalleled, but life was easy and everybody seemed satisfied. Godfrey lived in happy contentment for many years, with his goats and his hens, meditating on the problems of free will and immortality, upon which he wrote me lengthy screeds at irregular intervals. One morning he went out to blow up a tree root with a charge of dynamite, to get more space for his hens and goats. The dynamite exploded prematurely, and poor Godfrey was blown up with the tree stump."

Mephy was very tall, with a lean body, high-domed forehead, hair that was long and dark, and an expression that was mournful. He had inherited three thousand pounds from an aunt, and in those days that was a vast sum that gave Mephy a small but steady income on which he could live while wondering which of his many ambitions to fulfil. In the end, after trying Shakespaerean acting, he bought a herbalist's shop on the Isle of Wight.

Dreamy and ambitious, Mephy admired John with his far more active mind, and a deep and lasting friendship existed between them. It was through Mephy that John went to Hastings, where he was to invent television.

II. *Undersocks, romance and jam*

When war broke out in 1914 most young men with ideals went to enlist in the army and John did so too. The medical officer at the recruiting centre in Glasgow took one look at his narrow and skinny chest, by questioning found out his long history of colds and chills, and classified him as "Unfit for any service". For John this was rejection by his country. He remembered it all his life. To subsequent rejections it added bitterness.

He had to look for a job. He found a permanent job with the Clyde Valley Electrical Company. The pay was thirty shillings a week and the post was assistant mains engineer. What he had to do as an assistant mains engineer was to go outdoors, day or night, whatever the weather, and supervise the repair of any electrical failure in the Rutherglen area of Glasgow.

He could be summoned by telephone in his room at any hour of the day and night and he had to live in his area of Rutherglen, which meant living in digs and away from the care of his mother and the security of *The Lodge*.

Whenever an electrical failure occurred John had to assemble his gang of toughs – most of them were Irish navvies – and go out, often in the dark, cold and wet, and tramp along until he found where the trouble was, have the street dug up, and correct the fault. He could remember standing whole nights in the rain, cold and miserable, while Stibbs, the chief ganger, and his men dug holes in the roadway to find cables that had become faulty; and trying to keep control of truculent Irish labourers at four in the morning, when they wanted to stop the job and go home, was neither easy nor pleasant. Sometimes the toughs would be drunk and fights would start. He remembered when Jimmy McGauchy knocked Billy Macilvaney down a manhole, both eventually going off with roars of pain and anger, cursing while the rain was driven by a biting wind.

The language and habits of the gang made a deep impression on him, and years later he used to enjoy imitating them to his more staid acquaintances.

Being an assistant mains engineer was the "steady job" which society advocated, and John hated it. What kept him going was the belief that his miseries were temporary, that life would improve, that he would break away from the slavery of long hours of work with not enough money. He even felt pity for his fellow workers who had no prospect of release, though at that time he did not notice that most of the men were resigned to their lot. They were not even socialists and they found relief in bouts of heavy drinking at weekends.

At this job John was constantly away ill: winters were a round of colds, chills, and influenza. Because of his constant absences there was no prospect of promotion and because there was no prospect of promotion he disliked the job. He stuck it out for five years.

One incident enlivened the five years of misery and was a first step towards finding other ways of earning a living, and that was using the technical amenities of the Clyde Valley Electrical Company in an attempt to make diamonds artificially.

He embedded a rod of carbon in concrete and then used the mains to explode the carbon. The mains fused. Expecting that this would probably happen, John quickly made good the damage, but in the excitement the block of concrete disappeared, so nobody ever knew whether the experiment in making diamonds was successful or not. But the experiment did make trouble for John and "difficult explanations followed".

The decision to leave the Clyde Valley Electrical Company

did two things: it shocked John's family and it showed that he could make money in business if he wanted to and really put his mind to it.

When he left the company his family were horrified that he was throwing away his expensive professional training. He felt he had no alternative, for even if he remained alive his spirit would be broken and he would lose the zest he had for experimentation. In 1919 thirty shillings a week did not amount to real poverty, especially if one had a loving family behind one. In later years, when John was known, the press made too much of the theme of rags to riches where he was concerned; the theme is always a facile and popular one.

His first venture on his own was the Baird Undersock, undertaken prudently before he left the company but probably a cause for leaving the company prematurely. His own feet were always cold, and he used to wrap them in paper before putting on his socks. He believed that socks were always damp, and even when I was married to him he used to change his socks two or three times a day. Paper undersocks were not commercially feasible and the Baird Undersock was an ordinary sock sprinkled with borax.

As John sold the undersock he quickly learnt how to sell and how to advertise.

In Vincent Street he took one room as an office and put an advertisement in *The People's Friend* announcing the Baird Undersock, medicated, soft, absorbent, keeping the feet warm in winter and cool in summer, at ninepence a pair, post free. He had one reply, enclosing ninepence.

As he had only his free Saturday afternoons to attend to this business he spent a Saturday afternoon as his own commercial traveller, selling two dozen pairs and obtaining orders for six dozen more. When he advertised again it was for commercial travellers to carry his socks. This new approach brought success, and he even sold some undersocks in London. But the most profitable field was Glasgow, for there he could supervise the business.

He found out that the Polytechnic, the leading department store in Glasgow, was not making a display of the undersock, so he sent in relays of friends to ask for the Baird Undersock. Undersocks boomed; other big stores wanted to be in on this successful line. It was the first time John's friends had helped him in business and it was not the last.

Then he learnt precisely how to use publicity. He wrote: "I began to get a little money together and spent some on publicity. I sent a squad of women round the town with sandwich-boards and got my first taste of what is known as editorial publicity. They were news, and photographs of them appeared in some of the illustrated papers with the caption: 'First sandwich women in Glasgow: new occupation for ladies'. The words 'Baird Undersock' appeared prominently on the placards. Some of the newspapers published this without comment, but in two cases I had to pay a small fee to have the name reproduced in the paper. It was first-class publicity".

But news of these activities in business were reaching the head office of the electrical company; to avoid the sack, John resigned.

The business was doing well. John added sidelines. Solid scent was one, Osmo boot polish another.

Then, in the winter of 1920, a really bad cold laid him low for six weeks and the business suffered badly. When he was well again he decided to sell out and go away to some country that was warm.

He sold the business to a man in Glasgow and was sixteen hundred pounds in pocket, an amount it would have taken him twelve years to earn with the Clyde Valley Electrical Company as an engineer.

As far as I know it was during the period of the undersock that John met the girl who was to be his romantic interest for the next ten years. He met her in a library, and soon they were deeply in love. His health was so poor that marriage was out of the question, and one of the reasons for going to Trinidad was that a warm climate might cure him. What he hoped for was a return to Glasgow with his health restored and his position in the world of business assured. He came back with neither and found that while he had been away the girl had married.

Trinidad, some eleven hundred kilometres north of the equator, is hot. Ten kilometres only off the coast of Venezuela where the Orinoco flows into the sea, Trinidad is humid; the vegetation is luxuriant, the insect life varied and rich.

Godfrey Harris had written to John and praised Trinidad. Guide books described the island as a Caribbean paradise. John filled three trunks with cotton samples and other goods and left Scotland – in a cargo ship, to save money. He had acquired confidence in his ability to sell goods; therefore he would go to Trinidad as a salesman.

During the voyage a hard-bitten Venezuelan inspected the samples and said that John had hardly any hope of selling the goods he carried.

He disembarked at Port of Spain and afterwards wrote: "The moist heat rose in waves from the crowded pavement. Negroes, Chinese, Caribs, Hindus, Portuguese, and a few sallow-faced Europeans jostled me on the narrow side-path as we walked towards the Ice House Hotel, where Harris had booked a room for me. I was glad to get there and lie down on the bare bed in the little carpetless bedroom. For the next few days I was very ill indeed. I had contracted some form of dysentery. Most Europeans got it sooner or later, I was told; I had not lost much time. It left me weak and miserable, with my faith in the Islands of the Blessed considerably shaken".

He began to try and sell his samples, and after three weeks

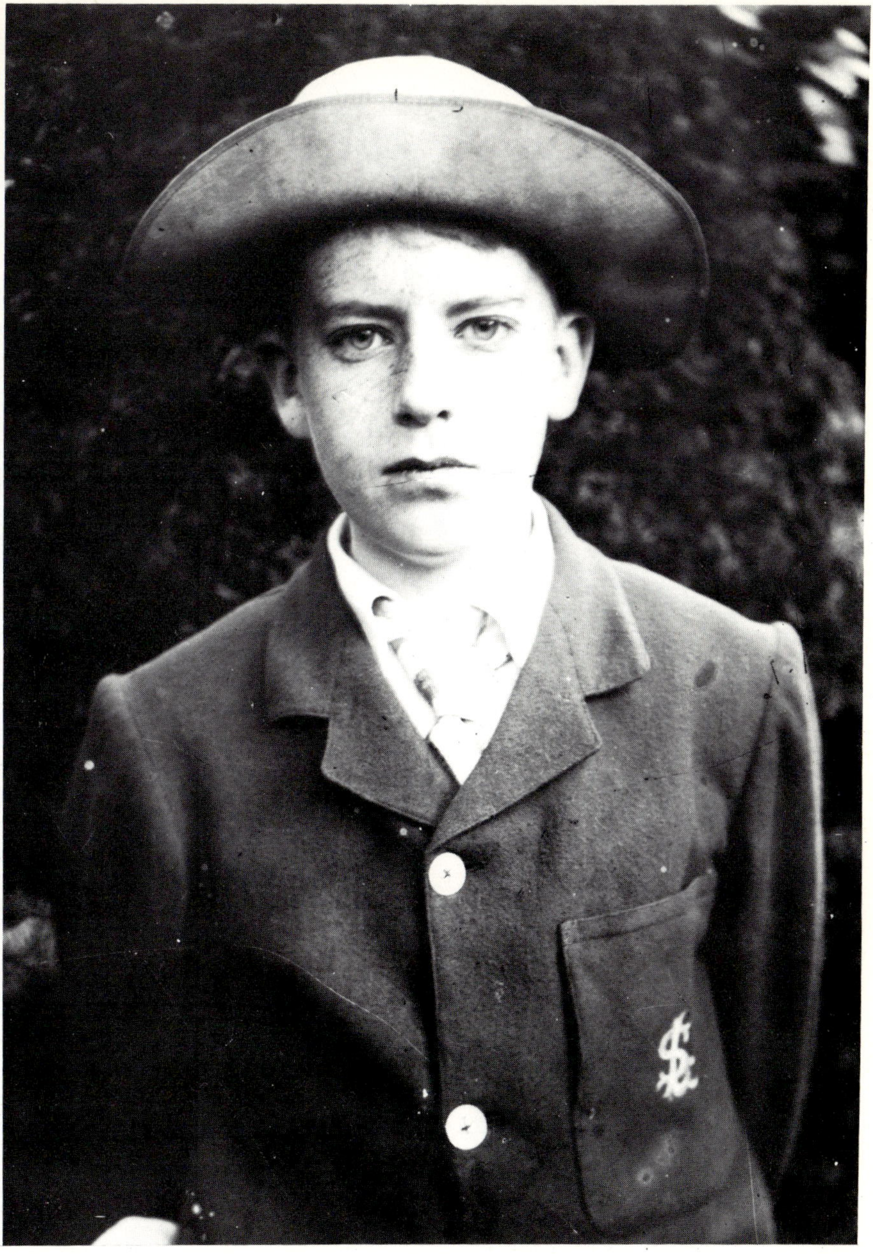

John Logie Baird, when a boy, photographed by himself. The undeveloped plate of this photograph was recently discovered by his son, Dr Malcolm Baird, developed by him, and the print made for this picture

John Logie Baird at the Rutherglen sub-station, Glasgow, in 191
he was then an electrical engineer with the Clyde Valley Pow
Company
(Reproduced by permission of Radio Rentals Ltd.)

The make-shift factory where John Logie Baird made jam in Trinida
(Reproduced by permission of Radio Rentals Ltd.)

his only sale was five pounds of safety-pins. Something had to be done, and quickly.

Ill in bed again, with a fever, he had an idea that seemed brilliant. The island grew great quantities of fruit: citrus fruits, guavas, mangoes. Why not preserve this fruit and sell it as jam? There was a fortune waiting to be picked up!

John did not rush into this venture without preliminary investigation. He found that the centre of the fruit-growing area was at a village in the Santa Cruz valley called Bourg Mulatrice. There he rented a room cheaply in a house belonging to the local cocoa-planter. He bought cookery books which told him how to make jams and chutneys. From a scrap merchant in Port of Spain he bought a large copper pan, originally a wash tub and big enough to hold a hundredweight of jam.

Everything was moved to the house where he had rented a room. The house was wooden and built beside a small river; it was surrounded by gigantic bamboos and in the heart of the bush. There, with the help of Ram Roop, a Hindu youth, and Tony, a large and simple creature, he started to build his factory, mainly of bamboo.

Inside the factory they built a brick fireplace into which the cauldron would fit, cut up oranges and filled the cauldron with sugar and oranges in the proportions called for in the cookery books, and lit the fire.

John continues the story: "Ram Roop armed himself with one of the spade-like wooden stirrers and I took the other. I took off everything but my trousers. The sugar melted and jam began to simmer. As instructed by the text-books we continued to stir, and soon the sweet-smelling clouds of vapour rose from the pot and floated into the jungle.

"They acted like a trumpet call to the insect life. A mass of insects of all shapes and sizes appeared out of the bush in terrifying numbers. They flew into the steam above the cauldron in their thousands, and, scorched, fell lifeless into the boiling jam. I dropped my stirrer and ran, but Ram Roop did not seem the least perturbed. After the first wild charge the insect stream abated a little, and finally we finished our boiling of jam and poured it into a selection of jam jars.

"But I had calculated without the insects. The factory became an insect paradise. Hundreds of enormous ants invaded us and in one night made away with a hundredweight of sugar. The floor of my bedroom swarmed with insects, mostly enormous cockroaches. Great spiders ran up and down the walls. Weird insects whose names I did not know flew in and out in swarms. Mosquitoes continually enfolded me in a cloud."

While in Port of Spain John had met a very agreeable companion called Harold Pound, and for part of the time they shared a bungalow. They spent much of their time together drinking gin cocktails and whisky.

One evening John arrived to find Pound with a large whisky-and-soda before him and gazing with apparently alcoholic horror at an unbelievably large grasshopper which sat on the table gazing at him. He was immensely relieved when John confirmed that the grasshopper was real and not an alcoholic vision. They caught the creature in a waste-paper basker and kept it in a canary's cage to amuse the people who visited them. Fed on grass and whisky-and-soda it drank feverishly and died of *delirium tremens*.

With difficulty John sold some jars of jam and chutney to the local store, then he fell ill again with fever. Ram Roop and Tony carried on, with John giving instructions from his bed.

There seemed to be no market for the jams and chutneys in Port of Spain, and when he was able to move about again John decided to return to London and sell his goods there. He bought a large cask and a number of paraffin tins and packed them with mango chutney, guava jelly, marmalade, and tamarind syrup.

With this cargo he set out for London, more dead than

alive, and with three-quarters of his capital gone. Harold Pound travelled to London with him and did his best to warn him against building hopes about selling the jam and chutney.

John took a small office in Lupus Street and eventually sold the jam, which was not up to standard, to a man who made sausages. He was paid fifteen pounds and that amount, with the five pounds for which he had sold the factory, was his sole return for venturing into trading in Trinidad.

Une saison en enfer.

III. *Soap, more romance and television*

When John arrived in London from Trinidad he went to stay with his elder sister Annie who was a district nurse in Deptford, but suffering from the English winter he felt the cold more than ever, one night even pulling up the carpet to add to the bedclothes.

To Annie he put the choice whether he should try television again or whether he should invent a razor that would not get blunt. She thought that there would be more money in the razor. John actually produced a razor-blade of glass, but he cut himself badly with it and gave up the idea.

Mephy now comes back into the story. He was living in a boarding-house in Bloomsbury as what was known as a partial boarder, meaning that he had partial board of dinner and breakfast, for which he was paying twenty-five shillings a week. John rented an attic in the boarding-house, and what Mephy was occupying was a converted wash-house, damp but supplied with hot water from the original wash-tub.

It was John's first taste of this sort of life in a London boarding-house and he said: "The inmates were the most depressing crew I have ever met. There were down-and-out commercial travellers, wretched elderly women eking out an existence on small pensions or hanging on as milliners, stenographers, and so on, in constant fear of the sack."

John was to spend much of the rest of his life in one hotel after another, with varying degrees of comfort but the same impersonality. He grumbled about the drawbacks of such a life but it suited him because it left him free to concentrate entirely on his work.

His finances were the trouble: his capital had dwindled to about two hundred pounds, so he had to make some more money. In *The Times* there were advertisements under the heading Business Opportunities, and when he replied to them all sorts of characters visited him at the boarding-house. Some wanted to sell patent medicines, others wanted him to put up a thousand pounds.

Finally he took a gamble. He bought some Australian honey going cheap at the docks, sold it by post from the office in Lupus Street, and again started to make money instead of losing it.

Then he left London temporarily for Glasgow, and the cause was his lady friend. The news that she had married while he was in Trinidad was a terrible blow, but a blow that struck a man who did not accept defeat and did not know when he was beaten. In Glasgow he saw her again and persuaded her to go away with him. Her husband seems to have been complacent, and she lived between the two of them. She was with John in the early days of television.

Back in London John met Harold Pound again. Pound was eager to help and introduced John to an uncle who was anxious to sell his business, a small shop under a railway bridge and very damp; it sold fertilizer. It had plenty of storage space, so John bought the business lock, stock and barrel for a hundred pounds and took one of Pound's friends into partnership.

John began to sell fertilizer and continued to sell honey. The business prospered. Then he bought a share in a small business dealing in the dust from coir fibre. But the damp office beneath the railway bridge was too much for his health: he went down with his usual cold and had to spend several weeks in bed. The result was that the partners bought him out, paying him a hundred pounds in cash and two hundred pounds in shares in an oil company, the shares proving worthless. Those worthless shares were to have an effect, for thereafter John distrusted the stock market, which later prevented the proper investment of his savings.

Before he became ill he had taken a prudent step, insuring

himself against illness. When he fell ill, therefore, with this illness which lasted six months, the insurance company paid him six pounds a week. That money made it possible for him to convalesce at the Buxton Hydro, as the doctor had ordered.

Air that was clean and fresh was a necessity for John's health, and for the rest of his life he was to spend many months in hydros or walking slowly along promenades at the seaside, in an everlasting search for health. As for our children, he used to amuse them with his rendering of "Oh! I do like to be beside the seaside . . .", which was very true.

By the end of 1921 he was well enough to return to the foggy and grimy air of London, and he had a hundred pounds in his pocket. He found a cheap residential hotel at thirty shillings a week, where his room was a converted conservatory, not the wisest of choices. Mephy had gone to Hastings and there was no friend to concern himself with John's welfare. Sometimes John fussed extravagantly about his health, as in the matter of dry socks, but sometimes he was quite indifferent to it, especially if thereby he could save a little on what he paid for his lodgings. He had a streak of true Scots thrift, which could come to light as strange and penny-pinching economies in the midst of lavish spending.

But at that time economy was really essential. Then he found an opening – in soap. He answered an advertisement in *The Grocer* and met a man called Young who told him of a good line. They ordered a ton of pale yellow soap in twin tablets, wrapped, took an office at 13 Water Lane, and, with Young as manager and a stream of decayed commercial travellers on the road, John sat back and waited for results.

His words run: "After a few days orders began to arrive. Mr Young booked a few; others came from the decayed travellers. They arrived at the office in person, invariably demanding a small sum in advance, and so the business grew. I decided to spread out and take a warehouse, to buy in larger bulk, and store and despatch myself. The basement of a tumble-down house on the South Side was obtained for a small rental. I wanted Mr Young to take charge of this warehouse but, while agreeing, he insisted on having a boy to help him pack and handle the goods.

"So there and then I inserted an advertisement in an evening paper: 'Strong boy wanted to help in warehouse'. The day after the advertisement appeared, I got out at Mark Lane station and, as I approached Water Lane, was surprised to see what appeared to be a riot, with two policemen trying to restore order. The whole of Water Lane, up to the junction with Mark Lane, was one seething mass of 'strong boys' come from all parts of the land to 'help in warehouse'. I slipped into the office by a back entrance, pushed my way through the strong boys who blocked the passage, and banged and shoved at the locked door. At last it was opened by a white-faced and thoroughly terrified Mr Young. We engaged the boy at the head of the queue, put a large notice on the door, 'Job filled', and remained in a state of siege.

"For days afterwards strong boys hung around the Water Lane office. Glowering and muttering, strong boys banged at the locked door and threatened to break in. Strong boys waylaid us in the passages and in the streets as we scuttled in and out."

Business began to boom. They sold soap to hotels, boarding-houses, ship's chandlers, and street barrows. The great advantage of Baird's Speedy Cleaner was its cheapness; it had few others. It was mostly soda, with the content of fatty acid ridiculously small. What could they expect at eighteen shillings a hundredweight? Most of the customers were satisfied; there were exceptions.

To quote John: "One day a very vulgar and ferociously angry woman banged her way into the office. She carried an infant, pulled its clothes over its head, and thrust its raw and inflamed posterior into my face. The poor child looked like a boiled lobster. The wretched woman had washed the infant in a strong solution of Baird's Speedy Cleaner. I calmed her down and pointed out that the Speedy Cleaner was a powerful scouring soap for floors and the decks of ships and not a toilet soap for infants."

The business flourished. John began to import large quantities of soap from France and Belgium. Harold Pound introduced two young men and the group formed a limited liability company with an authorised capital of two thousand pounds, John delighted at being a director of a promising company and all set to become a magnate in soap.

One day Young reported that Baird's Speedy Cleaner, which sold at eighteen shillings a hundredweight, was being cut by a newcomer, Hutchinson's Rapid Washer, at sixteen shillings a hundredweight. So John thought: If I cannot rival Hutchinson, why not join him? He asked Hutchinson to come and see him.

As John said: "Hutchinson was a hearty and jovial young Irishman. We got on well together and came to the conclusion to join forces. We met that night and dined together at the Café Royal. We sat long into the night, drinking old brandy and settling the last details of our merger. I felt ill when he saw me off at Leicester Square tube station.

"Next morning I had a terrific cold with a high temperature. I got rapidly worse. Hutchinson appeared with a bottle of eau-de-Cologne and was thoroughly alarmed at my state. He called a doctor who told me that I must get out of London at once or he would not answer for my recovery."

Hardly strong enough to stand the journey, John decided to join Mephy at Hastings. Obviously he could not continue in soap and his partners bought him out, leaving him with about two hundred pounds.

This was the third time a promising business had been lost through ill health.

It was the winter of 1922-3. John was thirty-five. But he had gained experience in the commercial world, knew how to raise money by forming a company, and realized the value of publicity and the personal touch.

Leaving London for Hastings was not the end of the association with Hutchinson.

At Hastings television was invented.

At Hastings Mephy took John to the lodgings they were to share in Linton Crescent. John was very thin, had only his two hundred pounds and no prospects whatever. But the weather was kind and he spent the spring of 1923 sitting in the pale sunshine of the seafront or browsing in the public library.

His health improved. His lady friend arrived and joined him and Mephy at Linton Crescent. John even met her husband in an attempt to "discuss the whole thing", but the situation was one without solution. Neither would give the young woman up, so she continued to live between the one and the other.

What her arrival did was to stress the seriousness of the financial position. For John business was out of the question and he could not earn a salary, so he had to invent something that would bring in money.

His first idea, though ingenious, contained the usual element of farce. I let him speak for himself: "I decided to try pneumatic soles, so that people could walk with the same advantage that a car gains from its pneumatic tyres. I bought a pair of very large boots, put inside them two partially inflated balloons, very carefully inserted my feet, laced up the boots, and set off on a short trial run. I walked a hundred yards in a succession of drunken and uncontrollable lurches, followed by a few delighted urchins. Then the demonstration was brought to an end by one of the balloons bursting. More thought was needed."

Then he recollected his experiments with television. These had been halted before the war by the lack of an amplifier for the infinitesimally small current from the selenium cell. But now, thanks to Ambrose Fleming, later to become John's friend, and to Lee de Forest, such an amplifier was in existence.

John took a long walk over the cliffs to Fairlight Glen, thinking out a complete system of television, and returned to Mephy full of new life and enthusiasm. Over the raisin pudding at luncheon he broke the news to Mephy, who replied that he hoped that John would not "become one of those wireless nitwits", that it was better to stick to soap, that John was in no position to play about.

But wireless was the point. The war over, wireless was becoming a commercial proposition.

Mephy was prepared to help. That afternoon they began to assemble materials in John's bedroom. Items included a tea chest, an old hat-box, some darning needles, sealing wax, Secotine, a bull's-eye lens from the cycle shop, wireless valves from government stock going cheap, transformers, and many little batteries, joined by clips, to supply the current

From these objects John created an apparatus which transmitted not an actual picture but the silhouette of a Maltese cross cut out of cardboard, the first object ever televised. What made the apparatus important was its simplicity.

"It was a circle of cardboard into which two spirals of holes had been cut with the sharp end of a pair of scissors. A darning needle formed the spindle, and by means of bobbins this could be revolved. On one side a powerful electric lamp shone through the bull's-eye lens on to a little cardboard cross and cast a shadow. On one side of this revolving disc another tin disc with serrated edges revolved at great speed in the path of the light. The selenium cell, connected by an amplifier, was on the other side of the cardboard disc. The neon lamp glowed when the cell was illuminated and went out when it was in the shadow, so that when the apparatus revolved, it was possible to see on one side of the disc the shadow of the cross on the faraway side, a distance of two feet."

The whole apparatus, transmitter and receiver, was connected by wires and not yet wireless television, but John was on the right track in scientific and engineering history.

In 1884 Paul Nipkow, an engineer in Pomerania, had taken out a patent for the idea of the analysis and synthesis of an image for transmission in a single channel of communication. John, as well as C. F. Jenkins, used variations of Nipkow's idea.

In a public library John had found a musty and torn copy of a book in German called *Handbuch der Phototelegraphie*, published in 1911 and written by Arthur Korn, a physicist, in conjunction with B. Glatzel. This was about the only thing resembling a text-book that was available.

John's work, so far, was not unique. Rigneaux and Fournier d'Albe had transmitted spots of light in 1906, C. F. Jenkins was experimenting in the United States and was to succeed with silhouettes in 1925. Edouard Belin in France and Denes von Mihaly in Germany were working on what were called shadowgraphs. A. A. Campbell Swinton in Britain had worked out an accurate theory of television but had not put it into practice. John was to be the first person to send a recognizable picture with light and shade.

John was elated with the transmission of the Maltese cross, feeling that he was on the right track, but again there was the lack of money. He put an advertisement in the personal column of *The Times* and invited some reporters to see his invention.

The advertisement appeared on 27 June 1923. It said: "Seeing by wireless. Inventor of apparatus wishes to hear from someone who will assist (not financially) in making working model."

The demonstration to the press produced a paragraph in *The Daily News:* "Mr John Logie Baird, of Hastings, yesterday demonstrated a device called the Televisor which, he claims, solves the problem of seeing by wireless." This paragraph produced an unexpected result. In Helensburgh a member of the Reverend John Baird's congregation read it and persuaded the minister that his son's work could have world-wide significance. The father sent the son a present of fifty pounds.

John was grateful: the money helped relieve tension that had arisen in their lodgings because he was using his bedroom as a laboratory. He was now able to rent a room at No. 8 Queen's Arcade, above a shop which sold artificial flowers, and he moved his apparatus there, paying five shillings a week rent and happy in his experimentation.

More important, he was improving his apparatus. It came to look like a cobweb of wires, batteries, lamps, and whirling discs, giving much better results. He could by then transmit shadows of letters and simple outlines.

That advertisement in *The Times* caught the eye of W. J. Odhams, proprietor of Odhams Press, who thought it was worth investigating. He sent two experts in wireless down to Hastings to see for themselves. One was F. H. Robinson, editor of *Broadcasting*, published by Odhams, the other Captain A. G. D. West, at the time chief research engineer of the infant British Broadcasting Company, not yet transformed into the British Broadcasting Corporation, though Reith was the general manager.

They were impressed by the invention but doubtful about its use in practice, for it would transmit a shadow over a few feet and no more. John made the observation to them that the problem had been to transmit at all and that it was only a matter of time before transmission would be over any distance.

He offered Odhams a fifth share for a hundred pounds but Odhams declined the offer because he foresaw "a long-drawn-out period of anxious toil". But he arranged for Captain West to send some vital apparatus to Hastings, much to John's encouragement.

John wrote: "Mr Odhams was very charming. He gave me tea and entertained me with a respect and consideration which were as balm to the soul of a struggling inventor accustomed to being regarded as a dangerous crank. 'Well now, Mr Odhams,' I said, 'what kind of demonstration would convince you?'

"He said: 'If you could put a machine next door, seat someone in front of it, and then on the screen in this room show his face – not a shadow but a face – then I am certain you would get all the money you want. I am anxious to help and I have discussed this with West and Robinson, but we can see no future for a device which only sends shadows'."

IV. Electrocution and bribery

With his own room to work in, John settled down to experiment in earnest. Lance Sieveking, then living in Hastings, gives the following description of him, a familiar figure as he wandered along the front. "It was mostly his back we saw. He had his hands stuck in his coat pockets, staring at the sea. Then he would suddenly say 'Ah!', as if he had seen something, and turn and go quickly into the room in an arcade that he used as a laboratory. I did not know then who he was, but the barber who used to cut my hair told me that he was 'one of those inventor chaps'."

In January 1924 John was able to transmit his shadows without wires, producing wireless television of a sort. William le Queux, who lived at Hastings, became very interested in the work but could not help financially. But he wrote articles on television in *The Radio Times* and other journals. One of them ran: "A Maltese cross was first transmitted and was clearly visible all over a large room, standing out luminously from the receiving disc. Other outlines and letters of the alphabet were transmitted with equal success. My fingers, moving up and down in front of the transmitting lens, were clearly seen moving up and down on the receiving disc . . . Those who listen to broadcasting will be amazed at being actually able to see by wireless."

At about this time John's mother died suddenly of pneumonia. Jeannie was married, and Annie was nursing away from home. Mrs Baird did much parish and charitable work and neglected a cold. Annie, herself ill, was sent home from hospital on sick leave. Her mother opened the door to her, and Annie, as a nurse, saw that she was near to death. A doctor was sent for, but it was too late.

John failed to see his mother alive but went up to Scotland for the funeral. His mother was buried in the family grave at Helensburgh, where John and his father now lie beside her.

His mother's death was a great shock to John, and her self-sacrificing character became his ideal in women. I was rather a surprise to him, with my upbringing in a more independent tradition.

By April 1924 the financial situation was again desperate. Then on 3 April F. H. Robinson of *Broadcasting* wrote in *Kinematograph*, a weekly: "The images were quite sharp and clear, although perhaps a little unsteady. This was mostly due to mechanical defects in the system. Moving images may be transmitted by this means, and distance is no object, merely depending on the power of the wireless transmitter and the sensitivity of the receiver employed. It is possible that machine-made apparatus on the lines indicated above could be made for some fifty pounds, which could be capable of transmitting letters and words clearly many miles through the ether, and all that appears to be necessary in order to reproduce and transmit moving pictures is more expensive and elaborate apparatus. The inventor is confident that no technical difficulties stand in the way of the transmission of moving images by wireless. Undoubtedly wonderful possibilities are opened up by this invention, its very simplicity and reliability placing it well to the front of many of the various complicated methods which have been evolved to do the same work."

This article interested Will Day, who owned a cinema in London and a successful wireless business. He went down to Hastings and before long John was signing a document giving Day a third share in the invention for two hundred pounds! John was to bear all the costs of patenting and developing! But he did not care. He said: "I would have signed away my immortal soul for two hundred pounds and I was not going over the terms of a legal document." The invention of television had John in its grip.

In fact he was delighted. He rushed back to Hastings from

London, where the document had been signed, and he and Mephy celebrated with a dinner at Molinari's. What he wanted was to start a company with himself, Day, Odhams, and William le Queux, but the last two were unwilling to get themselves involved.

Experimentation went on. The day John got back with two hundred pounds in his pocket he decided to try a stronger current. In his own words: "Following Will Day's investment I bought several hundred flashlamp batteries and began to realize my dream of a two thousand volt power supply by wiring sufficient dry batteries end to end. Some days later I had finished this formidable task and was connecting the supply to the cobweb of wiring when my attention wandered and I received the full force of two thousand volts through my two hands. It was sufficient to cause death, but I was lucky. For a few seconds I was twisted into a knot in helpless agony and then I fell over backwards, breaking the circuit and saving my life. But I shall never forget the agony of those few seconds. Electrocution must be a terrible death."

The explosion scarred his right hand for life, but the flash of the light and the noise of his fall attracted a small crowd and a reporter, whose newspaper said: "Inventor pinned to ground by short circuit" and "Serious explosion in Hastings laboratory".

The landlord, Twigg, sent John a sharp note saying that all experiments likely to damage his property must cease if John wished to remain his tenant.

The work was going well and the note was ignored. Soon the two hundred pounds were exhausted and he had to sell a sixth to Day for the money to carry on.

Then Twigg, annoyed at receiving no reply to his note, went to the arcade and saw John still at work on his wires. A scene ensued in the arcade, with John eventually beating a dignified retreat, unaware that there was a large rent in his trousers until he heard the crowd laughing.

Twigg's lawyer ordered John to vacate the premises and

A copy of the original Baird transmitter, with the ventriloquist's dummy used for experimental transmission of the human face and the Nipkow disc

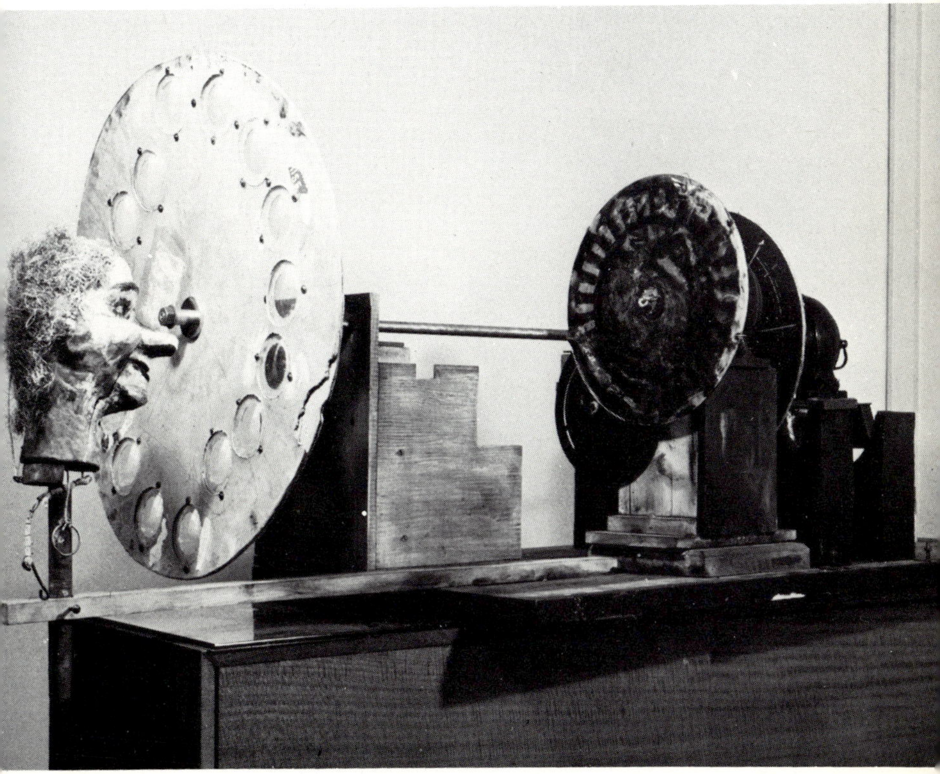

Baird's adaptation of the Nipkow scanning disc used in his experiments with television in the 1920s

(Reproduced by permission of the BBC and Mullard Ltd.)

this, according to John, "coupled with Will Day's and Mephy's urgent advice, made me decide to leave Hastings and transfer my laboratory to London".

His health completely restored he left for London in August. The original machine disappeared, perhaps sold for a couple of pounds to pay the rent. The wires and batteries went to London, and Twigg's property remained in peace until 1929.

In 1929 the Hastings Town Council inserted a plaque in the wall of Queen's Arcade, reading: "Television. First demonstrated by John Logie Baird from experiments started here in 1924".

John was at the ceremony, the mayor reading a letter from Sir Ambrose Fleming, who could not attend. The proceedings gave John much pleasure and this was one of the few tokens of recognition in his lifetime. There have been plenty of plaques since.

Will Day found John a laboratory in an attic at 22 Frith Street, Soho, and it was there that true wireless television was to be discovered.

The pace began to increase with the move to Frith Street. John had advanced from the transmission of shadows to outlines in black and white, sent from one room to another. He took out a patent for the machine. As Will Day now owned a portion of the rights, his name appears on the patent too – the first patent for television.

Work went on, John trying to get television by dividing the picture into a series of little sections of light and darkness and sending these in very rapid succession. To break up the pictures he used the rapidly revolving disc based on that patented by Nipkow. This was satisfactory because the eye saw the pictures as a whole with only slight movement caused by differences in the transmitting apparatus and the receiving apparatus.

The principal difficulty was light. In 1925 photo-electric

cells were so insensitive that they could only show the difference between darkness and a powerful arc lamp.

The result was that if he put simple shapes in the path of the arc lamp he could send their shadows, but to utilize the photo-electric cell for true wireless television, when all the light available would be the relatively feeble light reflected from a human face, was out of the question. It was the amount of light that was not adequate.

To get more light he built enormous discs. He said: "One disc was eight feet in diameter and had fitted round it spirals of bigger and bigger lenses, until I was using lenses eight inches in diameter. Light, light, more light! But soon I reached the limit. My enormous wheels almost filled the little laboratory, and as they had to revolve at an absolutely minimum speed of a hundred and fifty revolutions a minute, they were distinctly dangerous. The discs were made in sizes up to five feet in thick cardboard. Beyond that size I used three-ply wood.

"On more than one occasion lenses broke loose, striking the walls or the roof like bombshells. The apparatus would then get out of balance and jump from one side of the lab to the other until it stopped or tore itself to pieces. I had some exciting moments."

The other difficulty was money. John called at Marconi House, but Gray of the Marconi company was not interested. He visited newspaper offices and was treated like a crank. He advertised for a company promoter; there were so many replies that his lodgings at Ealing were besieged. Except for one, all the company promoters wanted cash for preliminary expenses.

That one, the exception, was Mr Brooks. His idea was to send a circular to all doctors, obtaining their names from the medical directory, asking whether they were interested in television. Three thousand circulars were posted and six doctors replied, subscribing in all seventy-five pounds. When Brooks had deducted his expenses there was not much left!

Will Day was beginning to wonder when he would see results; he would not invest any more money. He was to be bought out a year later, when television had become a flourishing business, but that was something which no-one foresaw in the dark days of 1925.

Money came from an unexpected source. In March 1925 Gordon Selfridge of the famous store in Oxford Street heard about television and called on John in Frith Street. There he saw a mask of white paper which could be made to wink its eye or open and shut its mouth by covering the gaps with strips of white paper. This was transmitted in outline from one room to the other room of the two rooms at Frith Street.

Selfridge had heard about television from a friend who lived at Hastings and he was looking for an attraction for his store's birthday week. He offered John twenty pounds a week to give three shows a day to the public in Selfridge's.

In April John took the apparatus to the electrical department at Selfridge's and there were demonstrations at half-past eleven, half-past two, and a quarter past three. People looked down a funnel-like arrangement and could see outlines of crude shapes transmitted a few yards only. John had also to answer questions.

My mother and I were in London at the time; I was a student at the Royal College of Music. My mother read about the demonstrations in the paper, as she was always interested in anything new, and we went to Selfridge's.

I must have seen John Logie Baird and his invention. Of him at that time I have no recollection. The invention had the effect which all mechanical things have on me and gave me a feeling of bewilderment and faint nausea.

But among the shoppers at Selfridge's were scientists and technicians. Dr Alexander Russell, F.R.S., principal of Faraday House and past president of the Institute of Electrical Engineers, wrote about the invention in *Nature* of 4 April 1925. Because the transmitting portion of that apparatus used at Selfridge's is now preserved in the Science Museum at South Kensington I quote Russell's account for readers with a scientific turn of mind:

"A series of demonstrations was given by Mr J. L. Baird of an experimental apparatus of his own design for wireless television (i.e. the simultaneous reproduction at a distance of an image of a fixed or moving object). The inventor does not claim any great perfection for his results, but we have seen the production in the receiver of a recognizable, if rather blurred, image of simple forms, such as letters printed in white on a black card, held up before the receiver. Mr Baird has overcome many practical difficulties, but we are afraid there are many more to be surmounted before the ideal television is accomplished.

"In the transmitting apparatus, the object, strongly illuminated, is placed opposite a revolving disc provided with a series of lenses, each a little nearer to the centre than the last, which projects a series of moving images upon a selenium or other photo-electric cell, each a little displaced laterally from the last. This is the equivalent of passing the cell over the whole surface of the object in a series of close parallel lines. The light thus reaching the photo-electric cell is rhythmically interrupted by a rapidly revolving slotted disc, and the result is that owing to the variations of resistance of the cell, undulations at an audio-frequency are produced in the current through it, whenever a bright part of the object is being dealt with. These are amplified and supplied to a single wireless transmitter, which is caused to emit corresponding signals.

"In the receiving section of Mr Baird's television apparatus the signals sent out from the transmitter are detected and amplified by very powerful valves, until they are strong enough to light up a neon tube when a signal is received, i.e. when a bright part of the object is being dealt with by the transmitting apparatus. A disc, with lenses or holes corresponding to the lenses of the transmitting disc, is rotated synchronously with the transmitting disc, causing spots of light produced by the neon tube to appear on a screen in positions corresponding to the part of the object being dealt with. With these means, a sufficiently recognizable image of the subject is produced."

The strain of three shows a day with this rickety apparatus and answering all the questions was too much and John was ill for several weeks. But the venture at Selfridge's produced money and the machine went back to Frith Street and more work.

John was not the only person working at television. In Britain his chief rival was Dr Edmund Edward Fournier d'Albe, the physicist, who on 24 May 1923 had transmitted the first wireless picture broadcast from London, claiming to be a wireless picture but not a wireless television picture. In the United States Charles F. Jenkins was transmitting silhouettes in July 1925.

Nor was John isolated in his attic, even if some people thought he was a crank. His air of quiet conviction and his certainty of eventual success inspired confidence.

Shortly after the demonstrations at Selfridge's a man called at Frith Street. He said he represented Hart's Accumulators and asked whether John wanted any batteries. They talked the matter over and John found that what he wanted would cost about two hundred pounds, while all he could afford to spend was ten pounds. A few days later he was surprised to get a letter from the managing director of the Hart company saying that the company wanted to encourage his pioneer work and had decided to make him a present of batteries worth two hundred pounds! That was a bright spot in somewhat anxious days.

But the Hart company was not alone in generosity. To quote John: "Shortly after this the General Electric Company gave me a present of two hundred pounds' worth of valves, which were infinitely useful. The enterprise of these firms was rewarded later when we bought thousands of pounds' worth of their valves and batteries. But for hard-headed business men to give two hundred pounds' worth of goods to a dilapidated and penniless crank in a garret was worth recording."

Then Scotland intervened and saved the day. John's mother was an Inglis, and the Inglis family were wealthy shipbuilders. The family had been following John's career with interest and, realizing that he was on the brink of a great discovery, they subscribed five hundred pounds for shares in a company to be known as Television Limited. John had his company at last! With this behind him he could confine his concentration to his engineering problems.

Light was still the main problem. After using the enormous lenses to improve the response of the photo-electric cell and failing, he decided to return to the selenium cell. But the selenium cell had a property which suggested that it could not be used for television, though it was far more sensitive to light than the photo-electric cell. This property of the selenium cell was that it took a little time to respond to changes in light. The result was that the picture it was meant to be transmitting with clarity appeared on the screen as a formless blur of light.

The problem, seen in greater complexity, was the lack of sensitivity in the photo-electric cell and the delay in the selenium cell's reaction to light. John studied the problems from various angles, including the physiological. He said: "I made a number of efforts to increase the sensitivity of the photo-electric cell and to find other materials which would give greater reactions to light. The light sensitivity of the human eye, according to Ederidge Green, and certain others, resides in a purple fluid in the retina of the eye and is called the visual purple.

"I decided to make an experimental cell using this substance and called at the Charing Cross ophthalmic hospital. Asking to see the chief surgeon, I told him that I wanted an eye for some research work I was doing on visual purple. He thought I was a doctor and was very helpful.

" 'You've come at an appropriate time', he said. 'I am just thinking of taking out an eye and shall let you have it if you will take a seat until the operation is over.'

"I was handed an eye wrapped in cotton wool, a gruesome object. I made a crude effort to dissect this with a razor but gave it up and threw the whole mess into the canal.

"My efforts to produce a sensitive cell without the time-lag proving abortive, I decided to try selenium cells and see what could be done to overcome the time lag. The first thing I tried was to use interrupted light by passing the light through a serrated disc which acted as a light chopper. Then the time-lag did not enter into the matter. The cell had only to distinguish between interruptions and no interruptions. I found that with this method I could use selenium for a picture, but the light chopper split it into coarse bars so that nothing could be seen but crude outlines. I therefore discarded the chopper and concentrated on the problem of overcoming the time-lag.

"As the object of my experimental transmissions I was using a ventriloquist's dummy. This head appeared on the screen as a streaky blob. What was happening was this: when the light fell on the cell, the current, instead of jumping instantly to its full value, rose slowly and continued rising as long as the light fell on it. Then, when the light was cut off, the current did not stop instantly but only stopped increasing and began falling, taking quite an appreciable time to get to zero.

"While watching this effect, it occurred to me that it would be cured or mitigated if I superimposed a curve representing the time rate of change upon the curve of the current with time. By putting a transformer into the current I should in effect accomplish this. The moment the light fell upon the cell there would be a change from no current to current. And although the current would be small, the rate of change would be great. Again, at the time when the current changed from increasing to decreasing, the rate of change would be at a maximum, so that I should get a big upkick and a big downkick when required.

"My amplifier, a source of infinite worry, was a direct-current, battery-coupled one. I decided to build a second amplifier battery. One amplifier could give me the time current curve and the second the time rate of change of current curve. I should then mix the two until the time-lag was corrected. I proceeded to do this. This, that, and the other went wrong, but I saw enough to realize that I was on the right track. But funds were going down. The situation became desperate. I was down to my last thirty pounds."

The best account of what happened then, the discovery of true television, is in the text of a lecture which John broadcast while in the United States in 1931:

"In 1925 television was still regarded as something of a myth. No true television had ever been shown, only crude shadows. At that time I was working very intensively in a small laboratory in the Soho district of London. Things were very black: my cash resources were almost exhausted and day by day, as success seemed as far away as ever, I began to wonder if general opinion was not after all correct and television was in truth a myth. But one day, it was in fact the first Friday in October, I experienced the one great thrill which research work has brought me. The dummy's head suddenly showed up on the screen not as a mere smudge of black and white but as a real image with details and with gradation of light and shade.

"I was vastly excited and ran downstairs to obtain a living object. The first person to appear was the office boy from the floor below, a youth named William Taynton, and he rather reluctantly consented to subject himself to the experiment. I placed him before the transmitter and went into the next room to see what the screen would show. The screen was entirely blank and no effort of tuning would produce any result. Puzzled and very disappointed I went back to the transmitter, and there the cause of the failure became evident at once. The boy, scared by the intense white light, had backed away from the transmitter. In the excitement of the moment I gave him half a crown, and this time he kept his head in the right position. Going again into the next room I saw his head on the screen quite clearly. It is curious to consider that the first person in the world to be seen by television should have required a bribe to accept that distinction!"

William Taynton was then working for Cross of Cross Pictures on the floor below John in Frith Street. This was a turning point in William Taynton's life too. John later employed him in his television company and he has been in television ever since.

In 1957, in the BBC show "This is your life", William said: "I didn't want to go but Mr Baird grabbed me, rushed me upstairs, and sat me down under some very bright lights. They were so hot that when he disappeared into the other room I moved away. In a moment or two he was back, looking terribly disappointed. 'It doesn't work,' he said. Then he saw that I had moved and gave me half a crown to sit still."

Television had been achieved. John was able to transmit a detailed living image. That day, 2 October 1925, was the first time it had been done. John was determined to reap the fruits of his invention himself.

V. Flicker and detail

Television had been achieved; John was able to transmit the living image in movement. It was the first time that this had been done, and he was determined to reap the fruits of the invention for himself. He knew that other inventors had not been able to develop their inventions for their own profit; he considered that his experience in business, making money out of jam and soap, would help him to make television pay.

He set out on a planned course, and to help him were Mephy, who had come to London and was acting as an amateur in Shakespeare plays, and William Fox, the journalist who had recorded the experiment at Hastings and was impressed by the way John obtained brilliant results from bits and pieces of discarded apparatus.

First, they had to convince the sceptical world of science that John had been successful in his attempt to invent television. The committee of three decided that television must be demonstrated to members of the Royal Institution: what they reported to have seen would not be disputed.

Second, there must be no delay in the demonstration, for John knew that others were working at television and could forestall him.

Third, the demonstration had to be successful, but care had to be taken that the large companies with investments in wireless would not take up television and use their vast resources to overtake and outdistance him.

John therefore repeated his experiments and issued his invitation to the Royal Society. Then, on the evening of Friday, 27 January 1926, more than forty members of the Royal Society, in evening dress and some with their ladies, arrived at Frith Street to find that they were expected to climb three flights of narrow stairs and stand waiting in a cramped and draughty passage.

Batches of six at a time were brought into the tiny rooms of the attic which served as laboratory. William Fox did his best to entertain those who waited or had already been inside.

John said: "In one room was a large whirling disc, a most dangerous device had they known it, liable to burst at any moment and hop around the room with showers of broken glass. However, it all went well. The whole assembly were given an opportunity to be televised, and I was certainly gratified by the interest and enthusiasm. The audience were for the most part men of vision who realized that in these tiny flickering images they were witnessing the birth of a great industry. I overheard one remark: 'Baird has got it. The rest is merely a matter of money'."

He was elated. This demonstration and many which followed established beyond doubt that his claim to be the first with television was true.

To add decorum to the demonstration of 27 January *The Times* alone, to represent the entire press, was invited to attend. On 28 January *The Times* reported: "For the purpose of the demonstration a ventriloquist's doll was manipulated as the image to be transmitted, though the human face was also reproduced. First on a receiver in the same room as the transmitter, and then on a portable receiver in another room, the visitors were shown recognizable reception of the movements of the dummy head and of a person speaking. The image as transmitted was faint and often blurred but substantiated a claim that through the 'Telivisor', as Mr Baird has named his apparatus, it is possible to transmit and reproduce instantly the details of movement and such things as the play of expression on the face."

Other demonstrations were followed by other reports, not all as dignified. Headlines such as "Magic in a garret" and "Young Scotsman's magic eye" did not inspire confidence in the scientific world.

The achievement of recognition was a continuous struggle against the current. John was accused of hiding a boy in a box behind the receiver and of all sorts of other tricks, accusations from people who had not seen a demonstration and couched in terms of innuendo and implication. When the facts made the critics change their words, they transformed their verdict from "it is a useless invention" to "anyone could have done it".

The Americans acknowledged his success in *The Radio News* of September that year. "Mr Baird has definitely and indisputably given a demonstration of real television. It is the first time in history that this has been done in any part of the world."

A few days after the first demonstration in Frith Street John was walking along the Strand, elated because he had just heard that Dr Alexander Russell was going to write an article on what he had seen at the demonstration. He was hailed by a familiar figure, Oliver Hutchinson, his former rival in selling soap.

"Hallo," said Hutchinson. "Glad to see you looking so much better. What are you doing?"

"I'm on to something really good," John said. "Come with me and I'll show you."

Hutchinson accompanied him to Frith Street and was given a demonstration. He was quick to see the possibilities of television, especially as John's monopoly was complete, and at once he joined Television Limited as business manager.

This pleased John, because if he had someone to develop the business side of television, someone to introduce a new and untried medium of communication to the world, he himself would be able to spend most of his time in the laboratory.

Hutchinson put most of his own capital into Television Limited and the Inglises bought more shares. Hutchinson became John's co-director. They bought out Will Day, who made a good profit, and they moved from Frith Street to Motograph House in Upper St Martin's Lane, where they took a small laboratory for John and an office for Hutchinson and, in November, were joined there by Mr Clapp as John's first technical assistant.

Hutchinson's task was to launch television, and the British Broadcasting Company, with John Reith as general manager, had not yet become the British Broadcasting Corporation, with John Reith as director general. The company was still smarting after battles for recognition with the Post Office.

Television Limited did not know how the broadcasting company and the Post Office would react to another and new medium clamouring for the use of the very few wavelengths then available. But the directors were confident, certain that once television established its claim, official help and encouragement would follow.

Leaving Hutchinson to get television on to a commercial footing, John concentrated on improving his invention, the first task being to make the lights on the person being televised less fierce and blinding. As he reduced the lighting he improved his apparatus, until he was getting good results with normal light, though the early pictures were quite unlike television today.

To quote John: "The pictures were made up from thirty strips. I found this to be the minimum necessary to transmit the human face. To decide the most suitable shape of picture to take in the face without wasted space I made endless measurements and ultimately decided on a long, narrow picture in the ration of seven units high to three wide. The number of lines was arrived at by making drawings from photographs divided into strips. I tried experiments with different numbers and came to the conclusion that thirty strips and a picture frequency of twelve and a half per second was the best compromise.

"The amount of detail was limited by the wireless transmitter which also limited the number of pictures I could send. It was a compromise between flicker and detail: more flicker more detail, but less flicker, less detail. My picture finally had a fair amount of flicker and a fair amount of detail, but was surprisingly good considering the small number of lines . . .

"With television established in the laboratory I was anxious to transmit over a distance and got in touch with Mr Kirke, chief research engineer of the broadcasting company. He was very interested and helpful and several transmissions were arranged, the television picture being sent from my laboratory to the broadcasting company by telephone line. Mr Kirke then put it on the ether through the company's wireless transmitter. I received it again by wireless at my laboratory. The picture came through practically unaltered and it is interesting to record that the company actually transmitted television in 1926, although unofficially. I was bound to silence and did not mention the matter at the time. It amused me to hear people say that while I could send television in the laboratory, it could not be sent over the British Broadcasting Company . . . The transmissions came to an abrupt end. Someone 'up above', Kirke would not say who, had ordered them to cease."

The decision to stop transmission was probably due to television's use of medium waves, the same wireless waves then used for broadcasting. Britain might have had television ten years earlier than she did if there had been more help and encouragement.

The company turned into the British Broadcasting Corporation, never a pioneering body. It could have arranged experimental television broadcasts after the wireless service had ended at night, something that was eventually done, but only after trouble and unpleasantness.

When transmission stopped, Television Limited applied to the Post Office for a licence to transmit television, and at the end of 1926 the licence to transmit television was issued. A transmitting station with its own aerial was erected on the roof of Motograph House and began transmissions to an experimental receiving station at Green Gables, a villa at Harrow. Radio amateurs used to be puzzled by the sound of "me-me-me" picked up at two hundred metres. It was the noise made by the transmission of television.

John was delighted with success; he worked as hard as ever but he began to enjoy himself. His friends included Mephy and Mr Clapp, a wireless enthusiast with an amateur transmitter at his home in Coulsdon, Surrey. With these and others John liked to dine at the Ivy and the Savoy. Such restaurants had to put up with his habit of drawing engineering designs on tablecloths and with his appearance, which was somewhat eccentric. With his long hair, horn-rimmed glasses, and massive overcoats he became quite a character in London. He enjoyed dressing the part of the absent-minded inventor and he was shrewder than he looked.

His private life was unsettled. His love affair was still in full swing, though both he and his lady were approaching their forties. His health varied with the seasons. In summer he was a reasonably handsome and lively man, but as winter set in he looked years older, his heavy black overcoat, even a balaclava, always on. Each winter he was in bed for several weeks with a chill.

He lived in various places. William Fox was living in Golders Green and John spent a lot of time in lodgings near him. When he wanted to be in town he moved to Brown's Hotel.

Mr Fox has said: "It was common for the doorbell to go at midnight and to find Mr Baird on the doorstep looking as though he had been dropped there and did not know how it had happened, or else he was bubbling with ideas. He would come in and sit for an hour without saying a word some nights; on others we discussed everything under the sun.

"During the day it was not unusual to find him on a public seat at the end of the road looking like a tramp, lost, weary, and half dead. He was not, of course, but merely lost in the depth of the details of some new idea . . . Time and place meant nothing to him when his ideas were moving."

But it is also possible that John was sunk in the Baird

lethargy which alternated with the furious energy with which he pursued his ideas.

Mr Fox goes on: "I found him a young man widely read, interested in many things but devoted to the idea of getting television on to a practical basis. To that end he worked in a fashion I have never seen in another man. His whole life and time were television. When he was working on a problem it was impossible to get sense out of him on any other subject. This was a peculiarity which puzzled many people and made them write him down as an impractical dreamer. But only a severely practical man could have taken up the bits and pieces of discarded apparatus and made them work to provide the answer to problems as Baird did."

During 1926 and the years immediately following John's ideas flowed in a rich stream and his inventions multiplied. Money began to come his way, the public company he had been dreaming of was formed, and he was having to deal with public figures brought on to the board of directors. With such figures he did not always deal successfully.

Ideas came so fast that he hardly knew which of them to develop first. People who know how his powerful competitors eventually outstripped him in applying commercial television sometimes say that it was a pity that he did not concentrate on the technical perfection of television. In saying this they lose sight of the character of the man, John Logie Baird.

For John the great thrill of television was ended when William Taynton first appeared on that screen, flickering and small. The rest, the "matter of money" as the visitor from the Royal Society had said, was less urgent. John had discovered how to make television work and he felt that anyone, for example his own assistants, could improve it to a commercial level. New and more fascinating ideas were calling him.

One example was the sound which pictures made on their wavelength, the "me-me-me" which puzzled the amateurs. He wrote: "In testing the amplifiers I used headphones and listened to the noise which the vision signals made. I became expert at this and could even tell roughly what was being televised by the sound it made. I knew whether it was the dummy's head or a human face. I could tell when the person moved. I could distinguish a hand from a pair of scissors or a matchbox, and when two or three people had widely different appearances I could tell one from the other by the sound of their faces, each face having its own sound.

"I had a gramophone record made of these sounds and found that by playing this with an electric pick-up and then feeding the signal back to a television receiver I could reproduce the original scene. A number of such records were made (one may be seen in the Science Museum, South Kensington), but the quality was so poor that there seemed no hope of competing with the cinematograph. If the cinema had not been invented, the Phonovisor, as I called the device, might have been worth developing." (It was only in 1972 that the video cassette, a sophisticated version of the Phonovisor, was introduced commercially in the United States.)

Inventions poured from his laboratories: Television, Phonovision, Noctovision, outdoor television, colour television, and cinema television. Many were merely slight adjustments of his previous inventions. For instance stereoscopic television was produced in 1928 by using scanning discs with two concentric spirals, one spiral dealing with the image seen by the left eye, the other with the image seen by the right. At the receiver the images were blended by viewing through a stereoscope.

He was seldom satisfied with a first attempt and he was working on stereoscopic television at the time of his death.

He produced four distinct methods of colour television. The last, the Telechrome, used cathode-ray tubes, the same system used by modern television. That was in 1934, a date which later on will become very significant.

The most publicized of these inventions was Noctovision, developed in 1926 when he was trying to reduce the amount of light on the subject being televised. He tried to dispense with visible light by using the invisible light at each end of the spectrum.

First he tried ultra-violet light and said: "At this time my only assistant was the office boy imported from Hutchinson's soap works. He was ignorant but amiable. The ultra-violet rays hurt his eyes, but he did not complain, but I got a fright and tried the infra-red. At first I used electric fires to produce these infra-red rays which are practically heat rays. I could not get a result and added more fires until Wally was practically roasted alive. Then I put in a dummy's head and added more fires until the head went up in flames.

"I decided to try another tack and used the shorter infra-red waves. To get this I used ordinary electric-light bulbs covered with thin ebonite which cut off all light but allowed the infra-red to pass. Wally sat under this without discomfort, and after one or two adjustments I saw him on the screen although he was in total darkness. That again was a thrill, new and strange. I was actually seeing the person without light."

The Germans used Noctovision during the last war, giving it considerable publicity towards the end in order to boost morale, both military and civil. In 1926, too, it had much publicity.

Dr Alexander Russell came to see Noctovision and wrote about it in *Nature* for 5 February 1927. "Mr Baird has now developed a method by which the image of the person is transmitted by flooding the 'sending' room with infra-red rays. On 23 November 1926 Mr Baird gave a demonstration to Mr W. B. Crooks and me. One of us stayed in the sending room with a laboratory assistant in apparently complete darkness. In the receiving room, on another floor, the image of the assistant's head was shown brilliantly illuminated on a screen, and all the motions that he made could be readily followed."

To develop television John needed money and facilities for experimental transmission. The Post Office licence, 2

TV, of 1926, gave the facilities for transmission, and money was provided by the Television Development Company registered by Captain Oliver Hutchinson on 27 April 1927.

Over the name of the company Hutchinson and John had their first quarrel, the first of many disagreements. Hutchinson wanted the name to be the British Television Development Company.

Hutchinson interested Ian Anderson, a partner in a firm of issuing stockbrokers, Vowler & Co. in the City. Vowlers, though rather nervous, were prepared to float a public company with a capital of a hundred thousand pounds or so if John and Hutchinson could find underwriters for half the amount.

John's Inglis cousins helped by taking five thousand pounds' worth of shares, and Hutchinson, who also had connections in Glasgow, found the rest, in all about thirty-three thousand pounds. Exact figures vary in different accounts of the entire business of the flotation.

Sir Edward Manville, chairman of the Daimler Company, was appointed chairman of the Baird Television Development Company. The other directors were Sir James Percy, Francis A. Shortis, John, and Hutchinson.

On 27 April 1927 the agreement to form the company was signed. On 28 April 1927 the newspapers were full of the news of a successful transmission by television from Washington to New York, the American Telephone and Telegraph Company having broken John's world monopoly.

The news caused Vowlers to feel that they had been cheated, but John convinced them that he was quite unaware that his monopoly in television would end so soon. He was even taken aback himself, though this development was only to be expected. He said: "Our demonstrations and the whole system, with drawings and details of our apparatus, had been given the widest publicity. Every big electrical firm had been aroused and their experts had been put to work. It was surprising that our monopoly had lasted as long."

Not many details have been given of the American system, but J. D. Percy, in a memorial by the Television Society after John's death, believed that it was virtually the same as the Baird system.

Although John now had his public company he was not at his best in the board room. Over the years various companies were formed and he went to all the meetings of all the boards, but he soon came to see these meetings as he had seen the church services of his youth – long rigmaroles to be slept through. He had no patience with the reading of minutes and the pomposities common in business.

Nor was he prepared to give details of his work to an audience which might be unsympathetic. William Fox, who joined the company to help with publicity, said: "He was very secretive, especially over his work, but in a most erratic way. He would, and did, most carefully conceal certain basic facts from his friends and those who were trying to help him, only to present them to perfect strangers who happened to come along and ask the appropriate question. Such actions naturally caused much difficulty and misunderstanding."

John was a scientist, only really at ease in his laboratory. He had to work out his discoveries by himself and resented interference while he was doing so. Sir Edward Manville, the chairman, was an engineer and tried to take an intelligent interest in television. He used to arrive at Motograph House without warning and ask what John called "innumerable pointless questions"; even worse, he would make impossible suggestions about how this or that should be done.

John could not stand Sir Edward's way, and when the company moved to Long Acre at the end of 1927 he had the door of his new laboratory made so narrow that Sir Edward, who was fat, could not get through without the loss of dignity and buttons. This did not make for the best of relationships between John and the chairman of the board.

John liked Sir James Percy, an old friend of Hutchinson's

and, like him, a genial Irishman full of good sense and good spirits; it was he who brought in Sir Edward, with whom he sat on other boards, and Shortis, a vice-president of the Guarantee Trust of New York. Unfortunately Sir James Percy died in October 1928. His son, "young" Percy, came to work for John and was a staunch friend and admirer.

Hutchinson and John had contracts with the company for five years at salaries of fifteen hundred pounds a year, more money than John had ever had. He wrote: "The Ivy, London's most luxurious restaurant, was opposite the office door, and there I tasted for the first time the joys of high living. Fine wines were introduced to a virgin palate and superb dishes of rich and strange foods to a stomach trained on sausage and mash. I plunged headlong into the joys of good food and wallowed there, all unaware of the terrible dangers that lurk in this apparently harmless pleasure.

"Hutchey and I lunched together: it was the high spot of the day. Commencing with cocktails, we went through the *hors d'oeuvres*, rich pea soup, *fritto misto*, curried chicken, and *bombe* Gladys Cooper, washed down with copious drafts of Château Yquem. Then we had coffee, *petits fours*, and old brandy, and, gorged, bloated, and belching, tottered over to Motograph House to await afternoon tea."

The pace was too hot to last. John's usual winter chill was complicated by disorders of the liver, and his nose swelled to twice its normal size. The days of the Ivy were over.

From then on he lived on boiled fish, soda water and toast. He developed chronic catarrh and the hobby of visiting specialists. The specialists recommended a variety of operations, but John had a horror of being cut about.

John's life had to be insured for what in those days was the very large sum of a hundred and fifty thousand pounds. As he put it: "My technical staff consisted of half-a-dozen new men who had not yet attained a mastery over the many weird devices which I then used. There were no television engineers in those days, and to the wireless experts much of my apparatus contained features entirely strange. After the formation of the public company the directors were much worried about this. They said: 'Supposing something happens to Baird: the whole thing would collapse.'

"So it was decided to insure me for a hundred and fifty thousand pounds. I was extremely unwilling and nervous about this. I remembered my war-time card, 'Unfit for any service'. If the insurance company turned me down, the directors might refuse to carry on. The chairman was adamant, so I was prodded about by two doctors who whispered together in a corner of the room. They obviously did not like the proposition. They were also reluctant to turn down such a magnificent piece of business. Finally, the insurance company decided to take the risk for twelve months at a whacking premium, two thousand pounds, I think it was. The situation was saved."

The company spared no expense. The staff grew, a lively and enthusiastic group. Wally, once the office boy, was put in charge of stores. Among the technical assistants were Mr Clapp, Commander W. W. Jacomb, the chief engineer from 1928 to 1935, Thornton Bridgewater (1928-1932), J. Denton, "young" J. D. Percy, A. F. Birch, D. R. Campbell, and J. C. Wilson, a brilliant theoretician who did much work on colour television before he died in 1941. Bridgewater and Campbell joined the BBC. Birch left for the cinema, the others stayed with John until he was forced to retreat to his private laboratory at Crescent Wood Road.

Life in the laboratories was not all jam. Hours and holidays meant nothing to John. No sooner was an idea past the experimental stage than he was on to the next, leaving the staff to perfect earlier ideas as best they could. Time was always too short for the capture of all the theories that flooded his mind.

Birch said of him: "In the same way that early radio waited for the thermionic valve in order really to progress, so unknowingly our J.L.B. awaited the cathode-ray tube to be harnessed to his inventions and make them commercially practical. He was always rather shyly pleasant to his staff and would enjoy a laugh with us on occasions. To myself he appeared very much the genius, with his untidy shock of hair and his spectacles. His prevailing fault, in our view, was a penchant for producing another idea for investigation before we had reached any sort of finality on the previous one."

John was always aware of his poor health, and it was that which gave him this sense of driving urgency. At any moment his work could be interrupted by a long illness, and he lacked the calm deliberation needed to develop a commercial idea; perhaps he remembered how illness had wrecked two careers in business. He concentrated all his energies in his laboratories, not worrying much about finance if there was enough to carry on with.

He often worked until three or four in the morning, wandering through the laboratories and masking his impatience with the mild question: "Well, have you anything to show me?" His good humour and courtesy made everybody like him, though he was not lavish with praise.

J. D. Percy says: "My most vivid impression of J.L.B. was his enormous toughness, underneath the quiet, dreamlike quality of his external personality. He would stop at nothing to achieve his end, which was always the furtherance of television. He had an unmatchable sense of humour and great courage, but I shall remember his resilience till I die. Underneath our professional relationship, affection was ninety per cent of what I felt for J.L.B."

Commander Jacomb was the chief practical interpreter of John's ideas and in the seven years he spent with the company he developed mechanical television to its limit. But the cathode-ray tube, which eliminated the need for moving parts, was the successful form of television, and John changed over to it too late to capture the market.

In 1927, however, that was far in the future.

Unaware of this cloud on a distant horizon John and his assistants worked until all hours, sleeping on the floor when they missed the last bus home, and living off snacks from all-night coffee stalls.

VI. Across the Atlantic

The years 1927 and 1928, full of incident, were probably the happiest in John's life because he had a laboratory with all the apparatus he wanted to satisfy the urge to experiment. The American transmission between Washington and New York having been a blow, he lost no time in preparing to retaliate.

Because that transmission had involved a large number of technicians and a distance of two hundred miles, he decided to double the distance and use no more than two operators, one in London, the other in Glasgow, more than four hundred miles away.

As the Americans did, he sent his pictures over the telephone line. Clapp went to Glasgow and set up his receiver in a room at the Central Station Hotel. Among those invited to the demonstration, which took place on 24 and 26 May 1927, was Professor Taylor Jones, who occupied the chair of physics at Glasgow University; he wrote about the demonstration in *Nature* for 18 June 1927.

This was not Glasgow's first meeting with television. On 3 February that year John had lectured on television at St Andrew's Halls, interest having probably been aroused by the publicity given to Noctovision. The Duke of Montrose, a wireless enthusiast, was in the chair and it was then that he compared John to James Watt and Henry Bell. On the platform, too, were representatives of the wireless trade, civic dignitaries, John's father, his sister Annie, and, of course the helpful Inglis family. For John the return home was a great occasion, and as for the Duke's remark, John said: "Even Papa was impressed."

The lecture was far too technical. The audience was dazed but enthusiastic. The Lord Provost, David Mason, proposed the vote of thanks, friends, admirers, and the press thronging the platform. John said drily: "It was an episode which would have delighted the heart of Samuel Smiles."

He continued: "I was now a celebrity, but instead of using this to get into the right circles, I turned down all sorts of invitations and continued to shuffle round in the lab. in a state of dirt and dishevelment, absorbed in my bits and pieces. I paid for my carelessness later on when big business got hold of television and myself. Oh, why didn't I cash in while the going was good?"

That rhetorical question deserves an answer in two parts. The first was his poor health and the need to concentrate on work instead of on a social life.

The second was his background for, like many a Scot, he could not make small talk with a lot of strangers, follow the nuances at business luncheons, drop a tactful word in the right ear. Like his outspoken father, he tended to despise the smoothly-spoken English and regarded their social life as a waste of time. To my cost I discovered that after we were married.

What he preferred was plain speaking, but few of the influential spoke his language, which had a disastrous effect upon his career. The lavish publicity he received did nothing to attract the scientific world.

Nevertheless, the formation of the Television Society in September 1927 was responsible for recognition, especially as it followed a successful demonstration of Noctovision at the meeting of the British Association at Leeds.

Doubts had been cast upon his ability to use Noctovision over long distances, so he replied with actions, which were louder than words. He and Denton installed a receiving and transmitting station in the municipal buildings and, on 7 September, staged a demonstration over the telephone wire between London and Leeds. They also transmitted pictures of members of the British Association from a dark room to a screen next door. Hutchinson made himself unpopular by keeping the queue moving in front of the screen, action inappropriate at a meeting of the British Association.

Some members of the British Association met at Leeds University and formed themselves into a society for the study of television, with Lord Haldane as first president and John as an honorary fellow. A bulletin issued to the press said: "At the close of a lecture on television . . . at Leeds University last night, a suggestion was made by a member that the time had come, owing to the enormous public interest and the success of Mr Baird's television development, for the formation of a society whose sole interest would be the study and development of problems associated with television and allied subjects . . . At a subsequent meeting specially convened for the purpose, forty-five signatories, mostly members of the British Association, unanimously formed themselves into founder members of the Television Society."

The following year John lectured and demonstrated at the British Association's meeting in Glasgow, and on 1 May 1928 he lectured at the first general meeting of the Television Society at the Engineers' Club in Coventry Street, London. Later on, meetings were held at University College in Gower Street, until the war stopped them for a time. In 1935 he delivered the first Kerr memorial lecture to the society.

Transmission between London and Glasgow had not satisfied John's desire to outdo the Americans and all through 1927 he worked in secret for a transmission across the Atlantic. Clapp, as an amateur, had a transmitter at his home at Coulsdon in Surrey and was in touch with another amateur, a Mr Hart, who had a transmitter at Hartsdale, near New York. John was determined to use this link between Coulsdon and Hartsdale for the first transmission of television across the Atlantic.

In August 1927 Clapp left for America and Hartsdale to prepare for the reception of television there, and John began sending his "sounds" of pictures, translated into wireless waves. John and Denton spent night after night at Motograph House listening to the whirr of the transmitter, for the only time the work could be done was after midnight.

Troubles arose. Clapp cabled to say that the tuning fork for synchronization generated curves which killed his reception; John cabled back and told him to remove his receiver to another house and connect it by telephone. That trouble dealt with, John found his signal too faint, and with great difficulty he and Denton increased the power of the transmitter.

While this was going on the company moved to bigger premises at 133 Long Acre, where they erected a couple of impressive masts and equipped a small studio for transmission. The transatlantic broadcast was to be one of Long Acre's great successes.

Soon Clapp reported from Hartsdale that he could see the faint image of the dummy on his tiny screen, and as the days passed the image became clearer and flickered less, In February 1928 John decided to transmit. Hutchinson had gone to New York, and he and Clapp waited anxiously for results. The first night was a failure. John had asked the actress Elissa Landi to come to the studio and be televised across the Atlantic; she was televised, but nothing was received in New York. The following night the signals were strong and Elissa Landi's place was taken by a Mrs Howe, who was clearly seen in America.

The Television Society issued a report: "There assembled at the offices of the Baird company in Long Acre a small party of press representatives and privileged guests. The transmissions commenced at midnight, London time, or seven in the evening, New York time . . . To give watchers at the New York end the opportunity to adjust receiving apparatus, the image of a ventriloquist's doll was first transmitted. The image sound produced by this doll . . . was sent over a telephone line to the company's private experimental station at Coulsdon. From this station the image sound was flashed across the Atlantic on a wave-length of forty-five metres.

"On the American side the signal was picked up by an amateur receiving station at Hartsdale, a suburb of New

York. After amplification, the signal was applied to the receiver televisor, upon the ground-glass screen of which the image appeared.

"Four watchers were anxiously grouped around the apparatus: Captain O. G. Hutchinson, the joint managing director of the Baird company, who had gone to New York to conduct the experiment, Mr Clapp, one of the company's engineers, Mr Hart, the owner of the amateur station a Hartsdale, and a Reuter's press representative. When the image of the doll's head had been satisfactorily tuned in, Mr Hart started up his transmitter, called a receiving operator at Purley, near London, and asked that Mr Baird should take his place before the transmitter . . . This message was telephoned from the receiving station to the laboratories at Long Acre.

"For half an hour Mr Baird sat before the transmitter moving his head this way and that until the message came through from New York that his image had come through clearly . . ."

The *New York Times* of 11 February had no doubts. It said: "His success deserves to rank with Marconi's sending of the letter S across the Atlantic – the first intelligible signal ever transmitted from shore to shore in the development of transoceanic radio-telegraphy. As communication, Marconi's S was negligible; as a milestone in the onward sweep of radio, of epochal importance. And so it is with Baird's first successful effort in transatlantic television."

Clapp and Hutchinson came back in the liner *Berengaria* and co-operated with the chief radio operator to receive pictures from Long Acre in mid-Atlantic. The captain and the ship's officers were very impressed, but most impressed of all was the chief radio operator. John had brought the chief radio operator's fiancée to Long Acre and televised her. On board she was clearly recognized, even on the tiny screen.

The shares of the company soared with all this publicity

An office was opened in New York. It was while John was investigating this side of the business that we were married in New York in 1931.

Vowlers, the stockbroking firm, were delighted with John's new successes and arranged to underwrite a new company, Baird International Television, which was launched on 26 June 1928. Lord Ampthill was chairman and Sir Edward Manville was on the board.

John still had no patience with board meetings. He and Hutchinson would agree in advance what they wanted the board to decide and then hope that the secretary would be able to guide the meeting in the right direction. John was hopelessly tongue-tied at such meetings and his few squeaks of protest would usually go unheeded.

Every evening at half-past eleven experimental transmission, under the licence from the Post Office, began at Long Acre. The Baird company made and sold receiving sets, at first on a very small scale, and slowly a public began to grow in London. The quality of transmissions gradually improved.

In 1928, too, John and Commander Jacomb improved the scanning in their transmitters and their receivers. They introduced the spotlight or "flying spot" principle, which enabled them to replace their heavy-lensed discs by simple discs of aluminium, fourteen inches in diameter, with a spiral of small holes around the periphery. The lighter disc simplified the manufacture of sets.

In the autumn sets were shown at the National Radio Exhibition at Olympia, but in Olympia itself no demonstrations were allowed. John therefore took premises near by and various celebrities were transmitted, including Peggy O' Neil, the actress. What with the transmissions across the Atlantic and the first demonstrations of colour television, achieved in the summer, television was right in the public eye and there was great interest in the exhibit and the new television sets, as they came to be called. John called the receiving set the televisor, but the name did not stick.

Among the journalists who visited the exhibit was Sydney A. Moseley, who was to become very important to John.

The two took to each other: John had found a man who spoke his own language. He described Moseley as "a stout and jovial man, with a merry and wicked twinkle in his eye, who immediately attracted me. He was to play a very important part in our future activities."

Moseley was immensely interested in television, took to visiting Long Acre, and was almost imperceptibly drawn into the Company's activities. To begin with he refuted an attack on television in a radio journal, an unfair attack verging on the libellous. Then he began to attend meetings of the board, where he was a great help to John, being anything but tongue-tied and wholeheartedly supporting John's ideas. He became "one of the family" and, in John's words, "was not the sort of man to fall asleep at board meetings or anywhere else where money was concerned."

Moseley was to become one of John's closest friends. They laughed and fooled about, as much in public as in private. John had found someone whose sense of humour matched his own and with whom he could relax. Moseley was no scientist, but he was a journalist with a shrewd knowledge of business and publicity and a real affection for John, evident in his biography *John Baird*.*

Throughout 1928 John was trying new things: daylight television was demonstrated in June, Jack Buchanan, immaculate as ever, posing in front of a transmitter fitted to the flat roof at Long Acre; the pictures were clear. In July colour television was demonstrated, beating the American Bell company's demonstration by a few weeks. *Nature* said that the demonstration was before the British Association in Glasgow and went on:

* Published by Odhams Press, London, 1952. Two short passages from the book are reproduced by permission of The Hamlyn Publishing Group Ltd.

"We have seen Baird's method of producing colour television. The process consists of first exploring the object, the image of which is to be transmitted, with a spot of red light, next with a spot of green light, and finally with a spot of blue light. At the receiving station a similar process is employed, red, green, and blue images being presented in rapid succession to the eye.

"The mechanism used at the transmitter consists of a disc perforated with three successive spiral curves of holes. The holes in the first spiral are covered with red filters, in the second with green filters, and in the third with blue. Light is projected through the holes, and an image of the moving holes is projected on to the object. The disc revolves at ten revolutions per second – ten blue, ten red, and ten green. At the receiving station a similar disc revolves synchronously with the transmitting disc, and behind this disc in line with the eye of the observer are two glowing discharge lamps. One of these lamps is a neon tube, and the other is a tube containing mercury vapour and helium. By means of a commutator, the mercury vapour and helium tube is placed in circuit for two-thirds of a revolution and the neon tube for the remaining third. The red light from the neon is accentuated by placing red filters over the view holes for the red image. Similarly the view holes corresponding to the blue and green images are covered by suitable filters. The blue and green rays both come from the mercury helium tube, which emits rays rich in both colours.

"The colour images we saw which were obtained in this way were quite vivid. Delphiniums and carnations appeared in their natural colours, and a basket of strawberries showed the red fruit very clearly."

Less successful was stereoscopic television, shown in August, but John continued to work at it.

Though these experiments produced no immediate results that were practical, John said: "What purpose was served by my effort? A very good purpose. Research was

The first photograph of a picture appearing on the screen of Baird's first apparatus for receiving television, called by him the Televisor

(Reproduced by permission of the BBC and Mullard Ltd.)

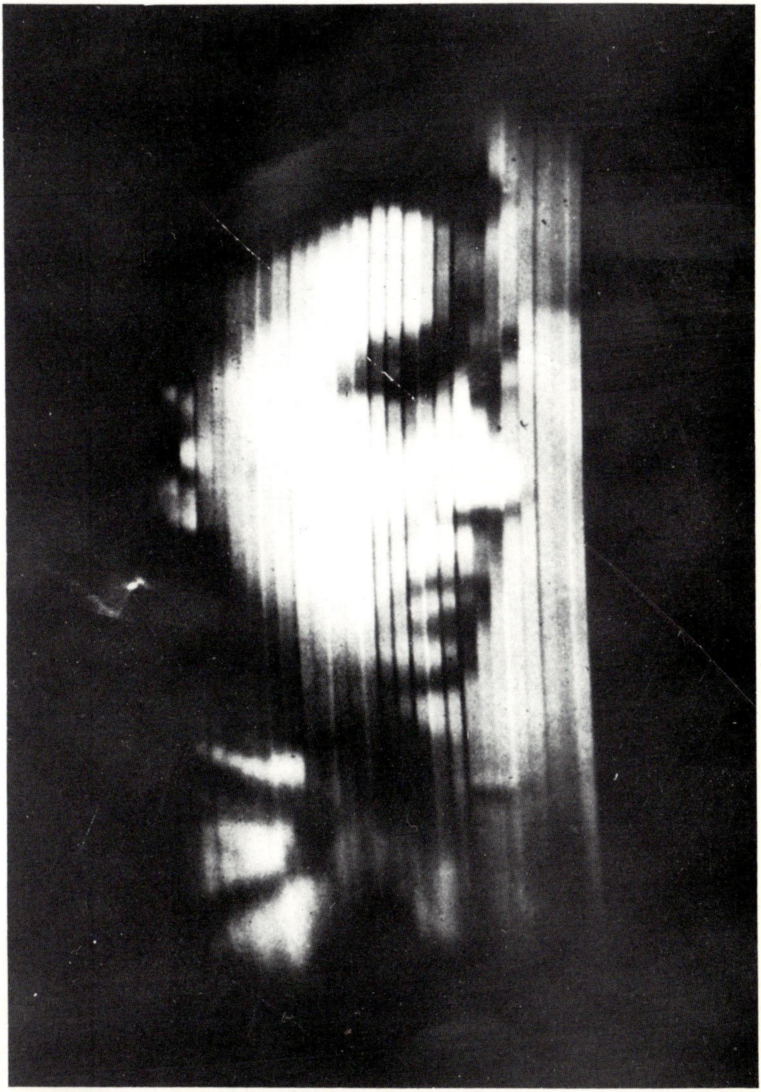

John Logie Baird and Margaret Baird

stimulated all over the world. Television *was* a practical possibility. These demonstrations stimulated progress in an incalculable degree . . . I was not interested in shares or money, but I felt I was doing something worth doing."

While the staff and the laboratory were a pleasure, the company was not. The investors wanted some return for their money. The company was selling sets, but on a small scale. All that the sets could receive was a picture of thirty lines transmitted after half-past eleven at night.

It was obvious that the company would have to obtain co-operation from Reith's BBC and transmit programmes a a more reasonable hour.

That step was not going to be easy.

VII. "How strange is the world"

By 1929 John had much improved synchronization, meaning that there was less flickering on the screen, and he was beginning to work on plans for a larger screen, Nevertheless, 1929 was a year of conflicts, difficulties, and conflicts resolved.

During the year a system of television was standardized for medium-wave transmissions on two hundred to five hundred metres, with a thirty-line picture and twelve and a half pictures a second. This system with low definition persisted until the BBC opened Alexandra Palace in 1936, when a system with high definition was introduced.

The Baird International Television Company was manufacturing sets with their trade mark, the winged eye, and gradually an audience for the programmes from Long Acre was building up. John said: "Regular transmission of television went on nightly from our Long Acre studio, our programmes were published in the press, and we were making and selling receivers. A large number of amateurs also constructed their own sets, so that in effect we had a separate broadcasting system, independent of the BBC.

"We sent out quite elaborate programmes from Long Acre, even including a little play, *Box and Cox*, and our transmissions were not only seen by the relatively small television audience but were heard by the general public if they tuned in to our wavelength, which many of them did." Well-known artists performed at Long Acre, more out of interest in the medium than for the nominal fee.

There were arguments in the board room about the best way to develop commercial television. Outside the board room critics increased the general discord, from ignorance or from annoyance at the success of an outsider. The BBC held a strict monopoly of wavelengths and would not allow more time on the air for the nightly television programmes.

John's main opponent was Captain P. P. Eckersley, chief engineer of the BBC, though there was nothing personal in the opposition, for they met and dined together when hostilities were over, John finding him congenial.

Eckersley, in his official capacity, was utterly opposed to the commercial use of thirty-line television. He thought it would disappoint the public because it could show no more than the head and shoulders, and he knew that making it effective would make greater demands on the medium wavelengths, already overcrowded. He failed to take into consideration John's energy and inventiveness. If he and John had co-operated, they could have achieved much.

Eventually John solved the problem by sending his pictures over ultra-short waves which transmit more clearly, though over shorter distances, and do not interfere with the broadcasting of sound. He also improved the quality of pictures, but that was not thanks to help from the BBC.

Technically, Eckersley's objections were correct, but the company had to fight for any transmitting time at all. Leading the attack was Moseley, and John was content to leave public relations to him, though Moseley did not understand technical difficulties. His attitude contained a romantic element, as if he were the champion of the lone inventor against the great corporation. But he gained for the company the transmitting time it needed to survive.

Moseley was firmly installed in the company, backing John in his disagreements with Hutchinson. Hutchinson, carried a long way on the tide of success, had ideas which bordered on the extravagant, seeking to take John's place at meetings of the board, and dreaming of financial deals that had more connection with a dream world than with the real world. In such circumstances Moseley's hard head was more than welcome.

Then trouble arose with the Admiralty. Long Acre was near the Admiralty in Whitehall. The Admiralty was another user of medium waves and complained that Baird's transmissions interfered with its signals. The television station 2TV was told to close down. But transmissions had to continue if the firm was to be a commercial success, so John moved the transmitter to Hendon, beyond the Admiralty's reach, and again approached the BBC.

Guided by Eckersley, the BBC refused the request for more broadcasting time. Eckersley seems to have been afraid of involvement with a commercial venture which by failure could damage the dignity of the corporation. The situation was not helped by an unfortunate incident one morning. The company's engineers were letting off steam in the studio with vulgar songs and rude remarks, and by accident the transmitter was on. The newspapers next day had headlines such as "Mystery station interrupts BBC" and "Mysterious vulgar broadcast". Though the source of the broadcast was not ascertained, the Baird company was suspected.

When the BBC refused him more time, John appealed to the Post Office. The Postmaster General, Sir William Mitchell-Thomson (later Lord Selsdon), had seen a demonstration at Long Acre and been impressed. He sent his chief engineer, Sir George Lee, and the assistant, Colonel Angwin, to more demonstrations. They reported favourably and recommended that the BBC give the Baird company facilities for television broadcasting.

Reluctantly the BBC fixed 9 October 1928 for another demonstration. Eckersley had warned the corporation not to expect much and the atmosphere was hostile. The BBC turned the request down.

John would not accept defeat. He saw the Postmaster General again, and a parliamentary committee was appointed to investigate. The chairman was Lord Clarendon, a former governor of the BBC, and members included Sir William Mitchell-Thomson, Sir George Lee, and Colonel Angwin. Sir John Reith and Admiral Carpendale, advised by Captain Eckersley and his chief assistant, Noel Ashbridge, represented the BBC.

With questions being asked in Parliament and by the press, the committee decided that the Baird company could have broadcasting facilities if a demonstration satisfied the committee, the Post Office, and the BBC.

The committee laid down rules for the experimental demonstration.

1. The Baird company was to install a transmitting station at BBC headquarters (then Savoy Hill) and transmit the programme through station 2LO.

2. The programme was to be witnessed on eight receivers of the type to be sold to the public.

3. Four of the receivers were to be at the General Post Office and viewed there by experts of the Post Office.

4. The other four receivers were to be at Savoy Hill and viewed by experts of the BBC and members of the committee.

The demonstration took place on 5 March 1929 and is best described by John.

"It was a nerve-racking ordeal, as we were to stand or fall by the result of one crucial demonstration. If a wire were to slip or a valve to burn out at a critical moment, the demonstration would fail and we should be faced by a devastating fiasco. The night before the test transmission passed like a nightmare on the top floor of Savoy Hill, trying to make sure that our transmitter would not fail.

"By morning all seemed to be well and I set out for St Martins le Grand (the General Post Office) accompanied by Sir Ambrose Fleming. Here in a large hall on the first floor, four receivers had been installed and soon, to my relief, they were running properly and receiving images of the artists we had assembled at the studio at Savoy Hill.

Mr F. W. Phillips, who was in charge of the Post Office's

arrangements, told the committee that we were ready, and they trooped in, headed by the impressive figure of Lord Clarendon. They took their places in front of the receivers and watched the little programme, simply consisting of head and shoulder views of singers and comedians. Captain Eckersley himself provided an unexpected turn when he went before the transmitter and was seen by the committee."

Among the artists at this test was Jack Buchanan, always ready to help the friend of his boyhood.

The show had been a complete success, but John awaited the verdict with some apprehension. It was more favourable than he expected, and he was very pleased to have been vindicated by a committee of experts after a rigorous test. From then on no-one could say that television was no more than a sort of trick.

The company received a letter with the committee's findings, but equally important the Postmaster General had a letter published in *The Times* of 28 March 1929, reading:

"In the Postmaster General's opinion the system represents a noteworthy scientific achievement, but it is not considered that at the present state of development television should be included in the broadcasting programmes within existing hours. He bases this view not so much upon the quality of the reproduction, which further experiments may be expected to improve, as upon the present limited scope of the objects which can be reproduced. The Postmaster General is, however, anxious that facilities should be afforded as far as is practicable without impairing the broadcasting service, for continued and progressive experiments with the Baird apparatus, and he would assent to a station of the British Broadcasting Corporation being used for that purpose outside broadcasting hours."

Added to the letter was a warning to the public that they bought television sets at their own risk because the system had not reached a stage advanced enough to warrant a place in the broadcasting programmes.

This was a fair judgment at that time and John was jubilant. But let him continue the story:

"The BBC bowed to the decision with very bad grace, did what they could to give us as small facilities as possible, and made conditions difficult for us. Hutchinson and I attended a conference at Savoy Hill, with Admiral Carpendale in the chair, where they offered us a quarter of an hour once a week after midnight. We were to pay all expenses. Long arguments and conferences followed, but time was passing and at last, rather than be held up indefinitely, we agreed as a preliminary to three half-hours a week from twelve midnight."

There was no final settlement until September, when a joint statement was issued: "The experimental broadcasting of Baird television outside programme hours will begin on 30 September. The object is to afford the Baird company wider opportunities than they have hitherto possessed for developing the possibilities of their system of television and for extending the scope and improving the quality of reproduction. In granting facilities for these experimental demonstrations in which the public can, if they so desire, take part, neither the Postmaster General nor the BBC accept any responsibility for the quality of the transmission or for the results obtained."

What may have helped final agreement was Captain Eckersley's resignation from the BBC, following his divorce.

A new era was showing signs of beginning in John's life, more in the technical developments than in encouragement from the BBC. He was beginning to travel, first outside Britain into Europe, then outside Europe into America. His income more than doubled and he began to get much enjoyment out of life.

Orders for television sets were pouring in and the tide seemed to have turned.

The first television broadcast over the BBC's station 2LO

took place at eleven in the morning of 30 September 1929 and lasted half an hour. Because one wavelength only was available, the divided system of broadcasting applied, with the performers televised only (in silence) for two minutes, then for two minutes the screens went blank and the performers spoke, broadcasting sound only, with nothing to view.

Moseley was the announcer, and the proceedings were opened by Sir Ambrose Fleming, F.R.S., (by then a firm friend of John's) who was followed by Professor E. N. da C. Andrade, also a Fellow of the Royal Society, as important in the world of electricity as Fleming, and by Major A. G. Church (of the Association of Scientific Workers), and a short programme of entertainment, among the performers being Sydney Howard, with a monologue, and Lulu Stanley, who sang. John himself had been persuaded to say a few words, one of his rare appearances on television.

A regular series of experimental programmes was broadcast by the BBC at eleven in the morning five times a week: they were of vision only. This was not done deliberately by the BBC; there was good reason, for there was one wavelength only available from Savoy Hill through station 2LO then on the roof at Selfridge's.

Reception was over a wide area. On 8 October 1929 the transmission was received in Bradford; John much preferred the medium-wave channels to the ultra-short wave transmissions which reached a small area. But short-wave television was to be the final standard because short waves gave better reception, pictures of more than thirty lines could be sent by short waves, and the medium waves were already occupied by other transmissions.

When the BBC opened its new station at Brookman's Park it allotted two wavelengths to the Baird company, which, on the divided system, broadcast speech and music on 356 metres and vision on 261 metres. The first united or dual transmission, broadcasting sight and sound simultaneously, took place at eleven o'clock in the night of 31

March 1930. It originated in the studio at Long Acre and was conducted by separate lines through the BBC's control room at Savoy Hill to Brookman's Park. On 1 April *The Times* reported:

"The programme yesterday consisted of introductory remarks by Mr Sydney A. Moseley, who is largely responsible for starting the present series of dual tests, followed by short speeches by Sir Ambrose Fleming, the well-known inventor of the thermionic valve, and Lord Ampthill, chairman of the Baird International Company. Songs by Miss Annie Croft and Miss Gracie Fields then followed. Mr R. C. Sheriff, who was to have spoken, was unavoidably prevented from coming to the studio."

Though John had acquired his regular transmissions, the situation was far from satisfactory. The company had to pay all the expenses of these transmissions, it had to maintain a large department at Long Acre to provide programmes, and it had to pay the BBC for the use of the transmitter. This was a high price to pay for publicity for the Baird sets.

Baird International was looking for openings abroad. In Germany the transatlantic transmission of 1928 had aroused intense interest. John said: "Dr Bradow, managing director of the German broadcasting corporation, came over to England accompanied by his two chief technical experts, Dr Bannertz and Dr Reisser. After seeing the laboratory experiments he invited us to send representatives over to Germany and install a transmitter in the Berlin broadcasting station.

"I found myself arriving at the Adlon Hotel in Berlin, complete with Hutchinson, a great load of apparatus, a team of technicians, and last, but dominating the whole picture, Sydney A. Moseley. Hutchinson had done the preparatory work and done it well. Our apparatus was erected at German Broadcasting House, the Reichsrundfunk, and a meeting had been arranged, to be presided over by the State Secretary of Posts and Telegraphs and to include Dr Bradow, the Postmaster General of the Reich, Dr Growirow, and all those interested in television.

"After this and other meetings a company was formed to develop television in Germany, under the auspices of the German Post Office. The Baird company was to supply the television, the Zeiss company to supply the television parts, the Loewe radio company to supply the wireless parts, and the Bosch company to supply the electric motors then used. Dr Bannertz, the chief technician of the German Post Office, was appointed consultant. This company was duly incorporated, the four concerns (including the Baird company) having equal shares, and Fernseh A.G. came into being. For some time we kept a number of engineers permanently in Berlin. I spent a lot of time there, and these visits were very happy until Hitler stepped in."

Hitler's rise to power was to change the position completely.

In 1929 the company rented ground at Coulsdon and set up huge masts through which they communicated with Telefunken of Berlin. There was no publicity and there was nothing political about the matter. A memorial stone, given by the Wembley County Council, was unveiled on 30 July 1953 by David Gammans, M.P., Assistant Postmaster General. The inscription on the stone reads: "Erected under the auspices of the Wembley Historical Society (chairman Councillor Martin J. Curley). This stone commemorates the site of the masts used for the reception of the first television signals from the Continent by John Logie Baird, pioneer of television, in July 1929."

In seeking orders abroad, negotiations took place with three French companies: Compteurs de Gaz, a private company run by Léon and Stoyanovisky, and the Pathé-Nathan company. For Compteurs de Gaz John built six transmitters which were installed at various places in France, but the negotiations petered out. Later, Barthélemy of

Compteurs de Gaz started his own system of television, no doubt based on what he had seen in London. John did not blame him after the way things had been muddled.

Léon and Stoyanovisky, with John, floated a French company, but funds ran short. The Pathé-Nathan company, a cinema concern, was induced to take an interest, but there money was short too, and eventually all French activities went up in smoke.

When Clapp returned from New York he headed an expedition to Australia, with demonstrations in Sydney and Melbourne.

Lord Angus Kennedy headed an expedition to South Africa, where he demonstrated television at the meetings of the British Association, held that year in South Africa. The first demonstration was at the University of Cape Town on July 22, the second a week later in Johannesburg.

Hutchinson's visit to the United States in 1930 was in the hope of founding a vast company there, and in 1931 he was followed by Moseley and then by John.

Hutchinson stayed on, always hoping for the big deal, but he could not pin any American down to a definite undertaking. At last he came back and all he had with him were some vague statements and a heavy bill for expenses. The board was annoyed, Hutchinson resigned, and he passes out of the story he entered by way of soap.

The company was pouring money out on travelling, transmissions through the BBC, staff, and equipment. It was hard to see how the shareholders were to be kept quiet.

But John retained his self-confidence. His salary from Baird International was three thousand pounds a year, a lot of money in those days, and he still drew fifteen hundred pounds a year from Baird Television Limited; his tastes remained simple. He had no holidays abroad and what he enjoyed was a week-end at the coast. He could not spend money on food, because of indigestion. All he wanted from clothes was warmth. Indeed, he remained picturesque in big coats, a black hat, and a fringe of hair down to his neck.

He would have gone on living in boarding-houses and hotels if Mephy had not taken a hand, ordering the domestic details of their two lives. He saw to it that John rented Swiss Cottage, at Box Hill in Surrey, for three years, furnished.

Swiss Cottage had once been the Duke of Marlborough's hunting-box, and Deepdene could be seen a few miles away. Although the house was only a few miles from Dorking, it could only be reached by a steep climb on foot from the town or by a road along the ridge on top of Box Hill.

It was twenty-two miles from London, but the distance did not matter. John's favourite saying had become "Money's no object", and he travelled to and from London in a hired Daimler. Mephy bought everything of the best, with cutlery from Mappin and Webb, a Scottish housekeeper, and a gardener. If Swiss Cottage was small it was also luxurious; in the drawing-room was an open fireplace in which they burnt huge logs all the year round.

Of life at Swiss Cottage John said: "While I was at home we spent happy hours tramping over Box Hill, discussing philosophy amid the trees, and recalling the past. When we climbed the bridle path leading up to the chalky side of the hill, Mephy strode ahead, a gaunt figure in a flapping black highland cape, his long grey hair floating in the wind, and grasping in his hand a great forked staff. One day we passed a lady and her little girl, and I heard her whisper loudly: 'No, dear, that's not Jesus'."

John had an electrical plant at Swiss Cottage and in August 1929 invited journalists and scientists down to a display of Noctovision, using it to detect objects in fog.

He entertained often and well, his guests being friends such as Sir Ambrose Fleming and influential men in the world of business.

When Lord Haldane died, Sir Ambrose became president of the Television Society; Sir Ambrose, born in 1849, was in

John's words, "a marvellous old man – his invention, the thermionic valve, revolutionized wireless communication, and in my opinion is by far the most valuable invention of the twentieth century . . ." (The valve was invented in 1904).

John hated being alone. If he had a free evening he would telephone a friend, usually Moseley, and send a Daimler to pick him up and, late that night, to drive him home again to Primrose Hill. After late nights in London John would take a taxi home from Long Acre.

On 17 July 1929 he gave a demonstration lasting half an hour to the Prince of Wales; he was terrified that something might go wrong and was much relieved when the demonstration ended.

In March 1930, after the first dual transmission (sight with sound) from Brookman's Park, the Prime Minister, Ramsay MacDonald, with the Labour Peer, the first Lord Passmoor, visited Long Acre and they saw each other on the screen. Ramsay MacDonald was also impressed by Noctovision.

John then installed a television set at No. 10 Downing Street, and, under the date 5 April 1930 the Prime Minister wrote:

"Dear Mr Baird,

I must thank you very warmly for the television instrument you have put into Downing Street. What a marvellous discovery you have made! When I look at the transmission I feel that the most wonderful miracle is being done under my eye. I congratulate you most heartily and send you my sincerest hopes for your future success. You have put something into my room which will never let me forget how strange is the world – and how unknown.

With kindest regards,
Yours very sincerely,
J. Ramsay MacDonald."

VIII. *In some way different*

The appearance of John's irresistible progress was contradicted by the reality of unsatisfactory meetings of the board following one another. John knew how precarious his position was; Moseley, a realist with money, told John that funds were once again dangerously low.

Yet to the growing number of viewers it was only a matter of time before all technical deficiencies were made up and a full service was established. The range of subjects televised was already widening.

To widen the range and to profit by publicity, on 14 July 1930 the first television play over the BBC was produced by Lance Sieveking, with Moseley as joint producer. The play was Pirandello's *The Man with a Flower in his Mouth*, chosen because it had three characters only. The cast was Gladys Young, Earle Grey, and Lionel Millard. (Val Gielgud, who was to have taken part, fell ill at the last moment.) They came to Long Acre and were made up in yellow, with navy-blue shading around eyes and nose, these colours on the face improving the picture.

Head and shoulders were all that could be seen, and each character had a turn before the transmitter. Not much of C. R. W. Nevinson's scenery could be seen. A select audience in a canvas "theatre" on the roof at Long Acre also saw the play on John's big screen, the screen soon to be demonstrated at the Coliseum and to have an influence on John's future.

In the select audience was Senator Marconi, invited by Colonel Winch, a director of Baird Television. John was as much impressed by Marconi's aloof politeness and almost regal manner as by what he had heard of Marconi's astuteness in business, so much greater than his own. Of Marconi he used words which could be applied with equal truth to himself: "Although the invention of no single device of fundamental importance can be attributed to Marconi, it was he who ventured forth like Christopher Columbus and forced upon the attention of the world the existence of a new means of communication."

Television was beginning to create its own conventions, and singers, violinists, lightning cartoonists, and anyone ready to appear came to Long Acre. The fees were one or two guineas, but the experience was novel. The make-up in blue and yellow horrified artists passing each other on the way to and from the room where they were made up. In the studio stood a grand piano; heavy curtains covered all the walls of the room. In one wall was a small aperture. The artist would stand in front of the aperture and perform into a blinding light.

The technical assistants took turns at announcing, keeping dinner jackets handy to cover enough of their working clothes to delude the viewers, who could see head and shoulders and no more.

None of this was profitable. The studio cost money to maintain, the company was paying the BBC for the use of the radio transmitters, and all the members of the board drew large fees. As John put it: "We were behaving more like a philanthropic institution for the benefit of the television-minded public than a business concern."

When Hutchinson resigned there was a short interregnum before Moseley was appointed business manager, a job he had in fact been doing for some time, undertaking all business with the BBC where he had a close friend in Gladstone Murray, one of Reith's subordinates.

Moseley made economies, even John having his salary halved. The number of television receivers sold passed a thousand, but funds still grew less.

Thornton Bridgewater, delivering the John Logie Baird memorial lecture at the Royal College of Science and Technology, Glasgow, in 1959, said: "Too much time was spent on adventurous sidelines and in exploiting the thirty-line system – largely in pursuit of publicity which, rightly or wrongly, was considered necessary for the attraction of public interest and capital. Too little time was spent on essential technical improvements."

But increasing the number of lines above thirty was not possible when transmission was by medium waves, and ultra-short waves were not yet in use. True, John might have started using ultra-short waves sooner, if he had not been inclined to leave improvements to his staff, who lacked his initiative.

Thornton Bridgewater continued: "I am now referring to the period after 1927, when a substantial company was backing Baird's work; it would be quite wrong to impute to him alone all the blame for the troubles. We probably have to accept the fact that even with the most skilful direction he would have had little chance against the large research organizations of achieving the profound technical advances that were necessary."

By 1931, the year I married John Logie Baird, the financial situation was becoming desperate. The company was saved by some clever financial moves by Moseley, who gives a full account of them in his book *John Baird.* The Depression was then at its worst all over the world, and money was scarce, even in the City.

John's account is simpler and goes: "The money we got from the sale of televisors was very small, trivial indeed compared to our outgoings, and it was obvious that some time must elapse before we could become a paying concern. The controlling shares were held by Television Ltd., the original Baird company which had been followed by Baird International Television, and Television Ltd. had been put into voluntary liquidation. One night, on the way home with Moseley to his house on Primrose Hill, I suggested that he should get some of his financial friends together and buy Television Ltd from the Receiver. The seed took root and

John Logie Baird at work in his laboratory
(Reproduced by permission of Keystone Press Agency Ltd.)

John Logie Baird and his son Malcolm in the house at Sydenham in 1938

Sydney got busy. By what devious financial wizardry it was accomplished I have never been able to follow, but by a succession of obscure financial somersaults Moseley got his friends to put up the money and himself got possession of Television Ltd. He did not write *Money-making in Stocks and Shares* without knowing his subject."

Moseley had worked hard to raise the money necessary to buy the vital block of shares. He failed in London and spent the summer in New York, in the fantastic atmosphere of prohibition and big deals which John and I were to experience a few months later.

Moseley got the money from Alfred Bates, a man in advertising and newspapers in London, paid out the shareholders, became the owner of Baird Television Ltd. and, ignoring offers from the United States and Canada, sold out to Isidore Ostrer, the poet and economist who controlled the Gaumont-British Picture Corporation Limited.

Where John's father was a minister of the Church of Scotland my grandfather was a rabbi. My mother was an Anglican of the High Church variety, my father, Henry Albu, unorthodox and liberal, going to the synagogue one day a year, the Day of Atonement, but quite willing to please my mother by taking me to church on Sundays.

I was born in Johannesburg in 1907. My mother, who had grown up in Yorkshire, had come out to South Africa in 1903 as a teacher, and here she had met my father who had left England for the diamond fields. He came of a musical family, related somehow to Felix Mendelssohn-Bartholdy, and three of his sisters sang all over the world with the Carl Rosa Opera Company.

By 1909, when my brother Gordon was born, we had moved from Johannesburg to Kimberley, where my father was one of the managers of De Beer's diamond mine.

Unlike John Baird, who at thirty-four had no vocation, at three I had mine. At a tea party I was asked whether I should like some tea. I shook my head at the hostess. "Would you like some cake?" Another shake of the head. "Would you like to go and play in the garden?" Another shake of the head. "Then what would you like to do?" This question brought a definite answer: "I should like to play on your piano."

In 1911 my mother took her two children to England to visit relations, but we children wilted in the climate and I received a gloomy impression of England which has never left me. As for Gordon, he looked so pale and wan that my mother soon took us back to South Africa.

We spent six months recuperating at Sea Point, Cape Town, and then my father became interested in alluvial diamond mining and we went to live at Klerksdorp.

Our house at Klerksdorp had a deep and shady stoep and an orchard; it was within sight of the Convent of the Sacred Heart.

I went to the convent, starting with French and German and, best of all, had lessons on the piano and in the theory of music.

At my first lesson I was not even allowed to sit at the piano. Dear Sister Lioba sat me down at a table, plucked a leaf from the morning glory by putting her hand out of the window, placed the leaf on the back of my hand, and showed me how to move my thumb and fingers, making a bridge of my hand so that the leaf did not move. But I was soon at the keyboard and began to pass the examinations of the Associated Board, always with honours.

When I was nine we went back to Johannesburg and I was sent to another convent. I went, too, to Miss Maude Harrison's Conservatoire of Music. Miss Harrison was a F.R.A.M. who had gathered forty certificated teachers of music around her, and among them they had more than four hundred and fifty pupils. I was there for seven years.

As my father grew older he had to go down from Johannesburg's six thousand feet to sea level, sometimes twice a year.

I, too, was supposed to have a weak heart, so the whole family would pack up and go to the Cape or to Natal.

When I was sixteen I passed my teacher's diploma of the Trinity College, L.T.C.L., and started to play in public.

Just before my eighteenth birthday it was decided that I should go to London. I did not want to go but I had little say in the matter, and in 1925 my mother took me to England. Her idea was to arrive in the spring, so I nearly froze to death.

My mother and I eventually took a small flat in Kensington. I hired an upright piano, horrid after my Steinway, and practised eight hours a day.

About the end of that year we went to Selfridge's, where John was demonstrating "seeing by wireless", but I remember no details of what I saw there.

In September I obtained my solo performer's A.R.C.M. and early the next year the L.R.A.M. Then I began to enjoy London, with a season ticket to Sir Henry Wood's promenade concerts at the Queen's Hall. Benno Moiseiwitch was my ideal pianist, and I heard Vladimir de Pachman in one of his last performances. Other memories are of Cortot, Thibaud, and Casals as a trio, of Madame Suggia, of Kreisler, of Heifetz, of Walter Geiseking as a rising star, Lotte Lehmann singing, Pavlova dancing.

I was back in South Africa from October 1926 to the end of 1927, by which time my dear father had died. My mother was then determined to leave South Africa, and it was with much reluctance that my brother and I had to accompany her to England.

The pianist Lev Pouishnov had vacancies for five pupils and after an audition he accepted me as a student. He charged what was for me a high fee, but when he realized this he sent me pupils who were not quite up to his own standard.

I began to get invitations to broadcast from Savoy Hill. Once, in 1930, I accompanied a singer in a television broadcast from the Baird company's studio in Long Acre. We were all introduced to John Baird in the studio; I was dead tired, as it was after midnight, and he was obviously thinking of something else. That was our second meeting. Our third meeting was to be different.

We moved from London to a house at Sutton in Surrey, and I played often with Sir Dan Godfrey's orchestra at Bournemouth and Julius Harrison's at Hastings. Sutton is near Box Hill, so both places had their associations with John.

In 1931 John was still at Swiss Cottage, Box Hill, with Mephy. None of his associates were really in sympathy with his work except Moseley, and he was away in the United States most of that summer trying to raise money.

I was twenty-four and beginning to get good engagements as a pianist. I did not find life in England congenial, but there were a few friends from home in London at that time, and one of them was called Grace.

One day Grace telephoned me and said: "I've been asked to go and have tea with a man who lives on top of Box Hill and I'd rather not go alone."

I agreed to go with her.

"It will be quite easy," Grace said. "He is sending a car for me. I'll pick you up and we'll be back by half-past six." Grace was an optimist.

The following Saturday Grace arrived in the car. Near Box Hill the chauffeur lost his way and it was not until he asked someone the way to Mr Baird's house that I realized who it was that we were to visit.

We arrived at Swiss Cottage and I was introduced to John and Mephy. We sat around the log fire in the drawing-room although the August sun was blazing outside.

Mr Baird was a tousle-headed man of forty-two, with wide blue eyes, a courteous manner, and an air, which impressed even me, of being someone in some way different from the majority of men. As the afternoon drew to a close he said in a voice that beseeched us: "Will you two girls give me the pleasure of coming down to Worthing for dinner? The chauffeur will drive you straight home afterwards."

He could usually persuade people to do what he wanted and the drive to the coast was pleasant in the clear evening.

As we climbed into the car after taking our leave he ran down the steps of Warne's Hotel and asked for my telephone number. Hoping that this meant an engagement for television, I gave it to him. His parting words were: "I wish I was returning with you girls instead of spending the weekend alone here."

The following Monday I was out teaching when my mother's maid, Doris, telephoned me, saying: "Oh, Miss Margaret, do be home by eight o'clock. Mr Baird has phoned you five times today and will be phoning again at eight."

I went home and took the call. It was not for an engagement for television but an invitation to dinner at Swiss Cottage.

We saw each other every day, and by the end of the week the die was cast. Although there was nineteen years' difference in our ages, although our backgrounds and upbringing were so different, there was instant sympathy between us. I knew he was loyal, without guile, and could give me the security and companionship that I wanted. As for him, he said I gave him a feeling of youth.

IX. *"But the horses could be seen"*

When Moseley sold out to Isidore Ostrer of Gaumont-British, John was delighted. After the discouragement of his relationship with the BBC he had turned to cinema television, and until he died he hoped that television with the big screen would become the most important medium of entertainment of this century, and by big screen he really did mean a big screen, for the screen he was using in July 1930 already measured five feet by two.

The big screen had been the plan, even in 1929 and 1930, when he was so taken up with negotiations in foreign countries. In principle the big screen worked in the same way as the small screen, except that a revolving brush, which switched the thousands of lamps on and off, replaced the receiving disc.

The big screen of July 1930 had twenty-one thousand flash-light bulbs in thirty vertical columns of seven hundred bulbs each, and each bulb was in effect a point in the picture, the picture being formed by those which were on or off, to give the effect of light and shade. With thirty vertical columns, the big screen still gave a thirty-line picture, but much larger and brighter.

The equipment for the big screen was built into a small caravan so that it could be taken more easily from place to place.

The Coliseum's booking agent was among those invited to see the big screen operating on the roof at Long Acre. He booked the big screen to appear at the Coliseum for three weeks, starting on Monday, 28 July 1930. It was billed as Baird British Television and was very successful, the Baird company making a profit of fifteen hundred pounds from its share of the takings.

Moseley, as director of programmes for Baird Television, booked all the notabilities he could to be televised from Long Acre. An announcer on the stage was in touch with Long Acre by telephone, and the audience was encouraged to ask the people seen on the screen to make particular movements, all of which could be seen. And the Lord Mayor, Sir William Waterhouse, televised at Long Acre, held a conversation with his wife, who was in a box at the Coliseum.

Although one newspaper said that the screen had a "musliny" effect, the show compared well with the early talkies; the sight and sound in television, broadcast simultaneously on different wavelengths, were synchronized better than in the early talkies.

Among the notabilities who appeared were A. V. Alexander, First Lord of the Admiralty, Ruby M. Ayres, Lord Baden-Powell, Herbert Morrison, Sir Oswald Mosley, Sir Nigel Playfair, Miss Irene Vanbrugh, and George Robey.

George Robey did his act in three media: alive in person, on film, and on television. He started his act on the stage at the Coliseum, and while the film was being shown with him in it, he took a taxi to Long Acre in order to finish before the television camera. As *The Daily Express* said: "Television obviously has a long way to go, but it was proved last night that its young Scottish inventor has something which will soon arrest the attention of the world."

It was not until January 1932 that Isidore Ostrer actively took over control of Baird Television Ltd. By that time John's relationship with the board was worse than ever. When we were first married, the meetings of the board were a nightmare for him, and he could be ill with nervous strain for days before a meeting. Years of dealing with unimaginative businessmen had taken their toll.

It was only Moseley – and I must say he often maddened me by his casual manner – who really understood John's aspirations. The board wanted to turn the sale of receivers into a commercial proposition, but John's interest was in the new and fascinating developments in his laboratory.

The work in the laboratory was going well. In March 1931 part of a film was transmitted, after the transmission in January of eight figures, full length, on one screen, using what was called zone television, an escape from the monotony of head and shoulders. This was achieved by dividing the screen into three sections and transmitting them side by side. This was the method used to televise the Derby.

In the ordinary transmissions there was an improvement in synchronization and the pictures became more stable. In August came the portable scanner, the forerunner of the modern television camera, capable of following the artist's movements.

On 8 May came the first outside broadcast, using a mirror drum instead of a disc, thus increasing the optical efficiency of the scanning system. The mirror drum was a drum with thirty mirrors around it, each at a slightly different angle, each mirror scanning a portion of the scene as the drum revolved. The subject was the street at Long Acre. On 9 May *The Daily Mail* said: "A *Daily Mail* reporter looked into the television receiving machine in a room at Long Acre and saw the images of people passing to and fro in the street below. There was considerable variation in the quality of reception, due to varying degrees of cloud and sunshine, but the panorama of the streets was there – small boys looking at the transmitting machine in the road, a white-coated seller of chocolates, and so on."

On 13 May *The Daily Herald* conducted the first interview on television. The interview was with Mrs Snowden, wife of the Labour politician. She had been a member of the first board of governors of the BBC. The interview took place at No. 11 Downing Street, where John had installed a transmitter.

In 1931 John decided to keep the promise he had made to the press the previous year, that he would eventually televise the Derby.

Moseley got in touch with his friend Gladstone Murray, an assistant controller at the BBC, and asked for time to transmit the Derby. The reply came in the form of the following letter:

"Thank you for the note setting out your proposals. As already intimated, the BBC is anxious to assist your development within the limits imposed by prior service obligations. Accordingly, you could not have the London regional wavelength for your vision transmission in connection with the Derby. It might be possible, however, to arrange for the London national wavelength, i.e. 261 metres, to be placed at your disposal for the television signals from approximately two forty-five to three fifteen on the afternoon of Wednesday 3 June, provided the following conditions were fulfilled.

1. That the speech accompaniment, which of course will not be broadcast, would be on a telephone line quite separate from any telephone line rented by the BBC.

2. That the BBC engineers would be satisfied in a preliminary test that nothing involved in this television transmission should in any way interfere with the normal service transmissions of the running commentary."

So, on 3 June, John took his equipment, including the mirror drum, to Epsom in a small van which he parked opposite the winning post. Cameronian won the race, beating Orpen and Sandwich, and the horses were seen in action intermittently, as far away as Kent. There was much interference and flickering, due, in part, to the BBC's decision to allow three volts only for transmission.

Of that Derby John said: "The reception was by no means perfect, but the horses could be seen, and at the time it created quite a sensation." It did indeed, and it also showed the difficulty of getting a free wavelength on the normal bands and suggested that stations would have to be established on the hills all over the country for transmission by ultra-short waves.

With increased interest among the public the BBC became more enthusiastic about television. It offered the Baird company occasional use of its Studio Ten, near Waterloo Road, as from August 1931. Then, on 12 October, Noel Ashbridge, who had succeeded Eckersley and become the BBC's controller of engineering, visited Long Acre, saw a demonstration, and was impressed by the improvements.

Noel Ashbridge wrote a report for Reith which reflects the attitude of the BBC at the time. It runs: "The first picture I saw was easily the best television I have seen so far and might be compared, I think, with a cinematograph close-up of, say, fifteen to twenty years ago. Were it possible for the ordinary public to buy an apparatus of this kind and run it without difficulty or undue expense, I think we should just have reached real programme value. At present the apparatus is not in a fit state to develop commercially, but there is, I think, reason to assume that this will follow in a few years' time.

"While not being very impressed by what Moseley said, because a good deal of it was contradictory, I was much more impressed by the technical results which I saw, because I now think a good deal of development has been made in the past nine months or so.

"We ought to take steps to carry on television transmissions and development by some means or other, including the Baird company. I would be inclined to encourage the Baird company to a reasonable extent in what they are doing now, because I feel that someone must develop television for broadcasting, and if they do it adequately, so much the better. If not, sooner or later the BBC will be forced to do it and at great cost to the listening public."

What the BBC then did was to buy some of the Baird equipment and with it televise several of the usual sound programmes for the small viewing public. The first of these transmissions by the BBC took place on 15 October 1931 and was of Jack Payne's band.

Weekly transmissions lasting half an hour followed, and the BBC was willing to increase them once it had surmounted the difficulty of finding free wavelengths.

John was encouraged by this interest and began intensive work on television which would use ultra-short waves.

To find and use an ultra-short wavelength was one of the reasons which took him to the United States that year, for over there monopolistic control of wavelengths was not in the hands of a single corporation.

When John went to the United States in the autumn of 1931, in search of a wavelength, he and I agreed that if he remained there any length of time I should join him. I learnt that Moseley considered, too, that the visit would benefit John's health and that John himself should investigate the state of the American branch.

So, accompanied by Walter Knight, Moseley's assistant, he sailed for New York. To a large extent I shall let him tell his own story.

"Our company in New York, called Baird Television Incorporated, was proving very expensive. We had to pay for costly offices and staff, and the only result was lengthy reports holding out hopes of big deals about to mature.

"The board, urged on by Sydney, decided to send me to the United States to investigate the position, and in September 1931 I sailed in the *Aquitania*. I had assisted in building this ship as an apprentice in Glasgow twenty years before.

"Among the passengers was H. G. Wells, and I was quite excited at the prospect of meeting a man who, in my youth, I had revered. Knight arranged a meeting, and I saw them advancing along the deck towards me. Wells was a substantially built man of medium height, with a cap pulled down over his eyes, utterly devoid of any affectation or any attempt at effect. He was an anticlimax after the magnificent Sir Oliver Lodge and the overpowering Sir John Reith. There was no imposing facade here, only a poor, vulgar creature like myself.

"We had a short chat about youth camps. I said these institutions appeared to ignore sex. 'Oh well', he replied, 'every Jack has his Jill.' That is all I remember of the conversation.

"As the ship approached the pier in New York harbour I was surprised to see a body of Highland pipers, marching up and down with great *élan* to the skirl of the pipes. These wretched men were a gang of comic-opera pipers from the Ziegfeld Follies, a misguided but enthusiastic publicity agent having arranged to give me a real Scottish reception. His plan was for me to ride with a police escort at the head of the procession to the Waldorf Astoria where I had the royal suite!

"I could not face it but slipped away and reached the Waldorf Astoria in a taxi.

"A few minutes later the Highlanders, who emanated from Czechoslovakia, Louisiana, and Hollywood, arrived at the hotel; it was an expensive matter pacifying them.

"The royal suite was overpowering, particularly the bathroom, an enormous hall with a black marble bath set in the middle of the floor and a profusion of sprays and showers and gilded W.Cs. The rest of the suite was full of press photographers with flash bulbs flashing and reporters taking notes.

"Encouraged by the publicity man they stayed on and on, and I got the impression that they were interested not in me and my work but in the whisky and food. At two in the morning the last of them had reeled or been carried out and I went to my gilded bedroom.

"The next morning at eight three business men joined me at breakfast to discuss a very important proposition. To me the proposition was incomprehensible nonsense, but they ate heartily and drank quantities of rye whisky. At eleven o'clock one of them collapsed on the couch as if dead, with glazed eyes. The prohibition spirit had got him, and he was taken away for the application of the stomach pump. This seemed a commonplace in business routine."

After this unpromising opening John was welcomed to New York by the mayor, Jimmy Walker, who kept on referring to him as an Englishman, in spite of the Ziegfeld Highlanders outside playing "The Barren Rocks of Aden".

Then John tried to do business with an American millionaire who was too busy to concentrate on television. "It ain't up to the movies," was all the millionaire's lawyer could say.

After the millionaire came a stream of men in big business. They all had grandiose schemes that were not practical, and they usually had their lawyers with them with contracts already drawn up. John was bewildered by the constant stream of visitors who came uninvited.

John hardly ever wrote personal letters, though I have two brief letter-cards sent from the *Aquitania* and complaining of feeling cut off, missing the telephone. When he had been in New York for three weeks he telephoned me and, with a touch of Scottish thrift, reminded me that the call cost a pound a minute. He asked me to come over on the next ship.

I sailed on the *Olympic* the following week but had some difficulty in disembarking at New York, due to some law about women travelling alone, something to do with the white slave traffic, I believe.

Just as I was expecting to be put on Ellis Island John came aboard and threatened the officials with all sorts of things, including Mayor Walker. I have no idea what good that would have done but it worked, and I landed.

John did not look well. He said he had not left his heated suite at the Waldorf Astoria for three weeks. He was afraid of the traffic in the streets and could not escape the relays of business men who assailed him.

I was bewildered by the situation, the only problem appearing to be his health. Walter Knight agreed that we should get him into the fresh air and we learnt of Coney Island with its esplanade, the Board Walk.

It seemed logical to marry at once, but we surprised friends, relations, and the Baird company, for we saw no reason to explain our decision to any of them. We had our arrangement that I should join John if our separation looked like lasting more than a few weeks.

We also had to cope with John's old love affair. It had become hopeless, from his point of view, but he was kind and loyal and did not want a violent and painful break with her. He thought he would hurt her less if he could write from New York and say that he was already married, and we spent several hours on our wedding day drafting this letter, until the room was a mass of crumpled paper. It was a waste of time. She read of the marriage in the newspaper the same day, while she was in a restaurant, and the news was a violent shock.

Walter Knight arranged for a special licence and got a municipal judge, Judge Murray Hearn, to come to Coney Island and marry us. John was quite ill with influenza and in bed most of the time. Judge Hearn found he had to bury someone on 12 November, so 13 November was our wedding day. We were not superstitious, John's birthday falling on 13 August and mine on 13 March!

John sent a telegram to Helensburgh saying: "Married Margaret Albu today."

Old Mr Baird exclaimed: "Margaret Albu? Never heard of her!" He was ninety by then and had long been retired from the ministry, while John's last visit to Helensburgh had been in January 1930.

The company was more stunned than was old Mr Baird; besides, it had heard nothing of the business of the wavelength. Sydney Moseley decided to return to New York at once, and his arrival was stormy. Brushing me aside and brandishing his brief-case he shouted: "John! What the devil is going on here?" That was my first meeting with Sydney. He cooled down a little when he understood the situation.

A few days on the beach and the Board Walk in the autumn sun did wonders for John, and all of us, including Moseley, returned to the Waldorf Astoria.

Walter Knight arranged a wedding reception at the hotel. I have a photograph of us with our guests at a horse-shoe table, and we look like a couple of sheep among a lot of wolves.

John said of this period: "I think my marriage caused a certain amount of resentment among the members of the board: they subconsciously felt, perhaps, that I was using the company's time for my personal affairs. Myself, I think that the marriage helped the negotiations, as there is nothing the American delights in more than a celebration of some sort. All our business connections in New York were invited to a magnificent dinner to celebrate my marriage and they certainly appreciated it."

At last the business meetings seemed to be moving towards a result. Donald Flamm, who owned WMCA, an independent broadcasting station in New York, was enthusiastic. John sent for the camera with which he had televised the Derby, and after many demonstrations and much talk an agreement was signed. WMCA was to begin broadcasting television in New York, using the Baird system!

The agreement was subject to a licence from the Federal Radio Commission and we went to Washington for ten days to give evidence before its wireless committee.

This is how the proceedings impressed John: "The complete lack of formality was astounding to one accustomed to the dignity and red tape of British procedure. Reporters, witnesses, solicitors, and a smattering of the public sat all together in a large hall. The commissioner was a very young man who looked only in his twenties; he lay back in his chair throughout the proceedings, gazing abstractedly at the ceiling. Everybody seemed to give evidence at interminable length, and when my turn came the subject had been so thoroughly exhausted that there was little left for me to add.

However, I did my best. The proceedings ended without comment from the commissioner.

"Donald Flamm was quite happy about it and told me that we were certain to get permission. He was right: the licence was granted. Feeling I had done a good bit of work I returned to London."

It was indeed a good bit of work, opening up possibilities of expansion impossible in Britain.

This American contract and the licence to broadcast appeased the board, for it had been critical of John's long and expensive stay in New York.

Then the Radio Corporation of America, one of the main broadcasting organizations, used a nominee for an appeal to the Federal Court against the decision of the Federal Radio Commission to grant the licence. The grounds of appeal were that no foreign or foreign-controlled company be allowed use of the air in the United States.

At that time television was not advanced in the United States. Twenty years later, in writing to Moseley, Donald Flamm said: "When we made application on behalf of WMCA for the right to broadcast with the Baird system of television in this country, there were only eighteen television stations in operation throughout the United States (of which several were 'portable' stations) and nearly all of them were on an experimental basis. They ranged in power from fifty to twenty thousand watts, and the scanning lines per inch were either forty-five or sixty."

The appeal was successful and the Federal Radio Commission withdrew the licence to broadcast. This meant that nothing had come of John's visit to the United States and that the money spent upon it had been wasted.

The board protested, so John agreed to pay half his expenses.

Shortly after our visit the Baird company's office in New York was closed.

In 1933 all programmes, except the experimental, were suspended in the United States.

We returned to Box Hill in the middle of winter, everything bleak after the central heating and dry air of New York. Although I was determined to be a good housewife, we had agreed that I should continue my career as a musician.

Mephy solemnly handed over the keys of Swiss Cottage and went to live in a boarding-house in Dorking.

I made a start as a housewife by checking all the household's account books, something strongly resented by the housekeeper, who had her own way of housekeeping. And when Mephy caught flu, she told me that if he died it would be my fault because I had turned him out of his own comfortable home. So swathing him in blankets and keeping him warm with hot-water bottles, I put him in a car and brought him back to Swiss Cottage and nursed him until he was well.

Mephy then moved on and eventually settled in the Isle of Wight and bought a herbalist's shop at Ryde.

On the top of Box Hill I was lonely, with John going off to London every day in his hired Daimler; the only way for me to leave the house was to slip and slide down the hill through snow a foot deep. For company I got a black labrador from the dogs' home at Battersea, but John did not like dogs and one day when I was out he sent poor Sambo to the vet to be destroyed. I still feel it was a cruel thing to do, but John had been a bachelor for so long that he was not used to considering other people's feelings. What is more, his father had dominated *The Lodge*, and no doubt he expected to do the same as his father in his own home. But I had been brought up in a very different tradition, where women were given every consideration.

Although John hated dogs he liked cats, and there was always a cat about the house, purring on his shoulder or being stroked by a stocking foot. Perhaps their independent spirit appealed to him.

January 1932 was an eventful month. Isidore Ostrer

began the new year by actively taking over Baird Television Ltd. and although John was pleased at first, because of his interest in television for the cinema, the changes Ostrer made were unwelcome. Two of Ostrer's nominees joined the board, Harry Clayton, an accountant, and Sir Harry Greer, a director of companies, who took the place of Lord Ampthill as chairman. John found that he did not see much of Ostrer, and when they did meet they did not always talk freely because John resented being some sort of an employee.

In that month, too, we left Swiss Cottage for a house in Hampstead, where life was pleasanter and we both began to settle down.

X. The rival

Vladimir Kosma Zworykin, a Russian-born physicist who had obtained his doctorate from the University of Pittsburgh in 1926 and who worked for the Radio Corporation of America (and later in England for a consortium of companies), had demonstrated all-electronic television to the Institute of Radio Engineers at Rochester, New York, in 1929. His invention of the iconoscope was gradually to change all thinking about television.

It was with a view to changing over from medium waves to short and ultra-short waves that John went to New York in 1931, and his thinking was to change more as the use of the shorter waves pointed towards more lines in the receiver and a change from mechanical television to electronic television.

It was a need to change from competition with rivals to co-operation among companies with a common aim that caused a merger among the competitors of the Baird company. But with Isidore Ostrer in control of the Baird company, nothing came of attempts by John and Moseley to bring the Baird company, too, into the merger.

With improvements of the Baird company's apparatus and techniques a change came about in the attitude of the BBC, a change for the good, though there was no real change in the attitude of John Baird to Sir John Reith.

The political structure of Germany changed and with it the fortunes of Baird television on the continent of Europe.

The years from 1931 to 1933, even to 1934, must be seen as inseparable, not broken up into discrete periods. It was early in 1931 that John, with his usual faith in personal meetings as achieving more than letters, obtained an interview with Reith. John stood in awe of Reith, and Reith, preoccupied with the detail of running the BBC, was not prepared to involve himself with the problems of experimental television. That meeting was not a success.

Then, with John's increasing success in 1932, another meeting of these two men took place. John's description of it, written more than a dozen years later when his health was failing and he was sometimes confused about the order of events, probably has elements of both meetings in it. He wrote: "Arriving at the BBC I was ushered into a little waiting-room, and after a few minutes the door opened and Sir John entered. Twenty years had elapsed since last I saw him, a young student of the Royal Technical College. The youthful, heavy lad had fulfilled the promise of his youth. It was an imposing presence which stood in the doorway, a large, gaunt frame surmounted by a grim, rugged visage, topped by an impressive, domed forehead which was rendered the more foreboding by a large scar."

"Sir John was affable and cordial and we talked for nearly an hour, he seated at his desk beneath a stained-glass window in the vast office. I think at the time he really wanted to be friendly; he offered to support a government grant to my company for the furtherance of our research, and we parted in very friendly fashion, but it was not to continue."

This account contains more of the second interview than the first, for it was in May 1932 that Reith offered to back John in an attempt to obtain a government subsidy of ten thousand pounds a year for experimental television. The sum could have been raised by adding a penny to the cost of all radio licences.

Sir Kingsley Wood, the new Postmaster General, turned the proposal down in June that year, probably believing that with the Baird company behind him John had sufficient resources.

All this occurred while John's work on ultra-short waves, essential for commercial television by the BBC, was continuing, and on 29 April 1932 he gave his first demonstration, on six point one metres. Waves less than ten metres did not interfere with the usual waves in broadcasting, but their range was limited to forty miles and the picture had to be transmitted from a hill or tall building. The first demonstration was from Long Acre to a receiver on the roof of Selfridge's and a screen on the fourth floor, for Mr Selfridge, still supporting the invention, found that it attracted the public.

This first demonstration of ultra-short waves televised Dame Marie Tempest and Leslie Mitchell. Leslie Mitchell said: "We were, I'm afraid, most inexpert, as at that time one had to stand rigidly in one spot, otherwise one's face bulged out of one side of the screen or the other, or one's forehead went over the top, or one's chin went below the screen. Dame Marie's comment indicated our reaction: 'Well, Mr Mitchell,' she said, 'I must say that your *voice* was reasonably distinct'."

The screen for that demonstration was small, twelve inches by four, and indistinct, with its thirty-line definition. The receiver was new, with Kerr cells and the mirror drum, giving a clear and steady picture even though of thirty lines. With ultra-short waves it was only a matter of time before definition was improved.

The BBC was impressed by this broadcast and even more so with the televising of the Derby on 1 June. The image was far better than that of the previous year, but the BBC was not told that D. R. Campbell, one of the assistants, had increased the voltage permitted on the telephone lines from three to thirty! It did no harm and cut out most of the interference.

The broadcast of the Derby was made through BBC stations and also transmitted by landline to a cinema, involving days of anxious work. John said: "I used the same van as the previous year for a much more ambitious experiment, and fitted up a large screen, nine feet by six, at the Metropole Cinema, Victoria. The transmitter was the same as that used the previous year and consisted of a large revolving drum. The picture sent out by the BBC was narrow and upright in shape, seven feet high and only three feet wide. To give a large picture at the Metropole I had three pairs of telephone lines from Epsom and sent out three pictures side by side. The three pictures thus formed one big picture on the screen at the Metropole, seven feet high and nine feet wide.

"The demonstration was one of the most nerve-racking experiences in all my work with television, second only in anxiety to the parliamentary committee. The night before the show we were up all night putting finishing touches to the apparatus, and when the great moment drew near I remember literally sweating with anxiety. The perspiration was dripping off my nose.

"A vast audience had gathered in the cinema; even the passages were packed, and the entrance hall and the street outside were filled with a disappointed crowd, unable to get in. If the show had been a failure the audience would have brought the house down and I should have been a laughing stock.

"All went well. The horses were seen as they paraded past the grand stand. When the winner, April the Fifth, owned and trained by Tom Walls, flashed past the post, followed by Dastur and Miracle, the demonstration ended with thunderous applause. I was hustled to the platform to say a few words but was too thrilled to say more than 'Thank you'."

From May the BBC had been preparing to take over the programme and start a regular service. There was an audience for it. John estimated that about ten thousand Baird televisors had been sold. Writing from memory he might have overestimated the number sold by 1932, and the truth probably lies at about five thousand.

It was a great saving for the company when it closed the studio and programme department at Long Acre. The BBC installed a Baird transmitter in Studio BB in the new Broadcasting House and prepared to run their own programme even more economically than John had done.

Eustace Robb was transferred from the gramophone department to become director of the programme. Douglas Birkinshaw, fresh from Cambridge, was sole engineer in charge. Birkinshaw found the job too much for one man and asked D. R. Campbell and Thornton Bridgewater, who had helped install the equipment, to join him. They did. John lost two of his best engineers, and both did well in the BBC.

The BBC's first broadcast was on 22 August 1932, John being introduced by Roger Eckersley, director of programmes and brother of the former chief engineer. John merely said: "I wish to thank the BBC for inviting me tonight and express the hope that this new series of television transmissions will lead to developments of broadcasting, increasing its utility, and adding to the enjoyment of the great listening public."

In September 1932 the BBC agreed with the Baird company to provide at least two programmes a week until 31 March 1934. In fact there were soon transmissions every week-day from eleven in the morning until midday, Eustace Robb trying everything from ballet to music hall, and they went on until September 1936, when they were superseded by high-definition television on ultra-short waves.

When the low-definition service closed down, the Baird mirror-drum transmitter was placed in the Science Museum at South Kensington.

In September 1933 John demonstrated high-definition television at the British Association's meeting at Leicester, using a receiver with a cathode-ray tube. This was a Farnsworth tube, the work of Philo Farnsworth, a solitary American inventor. John saw that the cathode-ray tube was the coming thing and persuaded Ostrer to buy him the right to use the Farnsworth tube. The picture had one hundred and twenty-five lines with twenty-five pictures a second and was five inches square, magnified to eight inches by a lens.

In July of that year he had fulfilled an old ambition and taken a lease at the Crystal Palace at Norwood. The company rented part of the ground floor and the south tower from the manager, Sir Harry Buckland. It was ideal for transmission by ultra-short waves, being one of the highest points in London. The Postmaster General granted an experimental licence and they transmitted images from one hundred and twenty to two hundred and forty lines on eight and a half metres.

It was in the Crystal Palace that they built and tested all the transmitting plant later sold to the BBC for ultra-short wave transmissions.

The experimental transmissions from the Crystal Palace were received at Film House in Wardour Street.

Although the BBC followed up its interest in ultra-short wave television by testing some of John's apparatus during the closing months of 1933, serious competition was at last making itself felt.

Competition and the need to go beyond mechanical television and a small number of lines, spending large sums on fundamental research and developing discoveries into practical applications which could be sold at a reasonable price suggested that the Baird company come to a compromise with larger organizations. It was becoming obvious that these organizations ought to be converted from competitors into partners.

All this time the BBC was watching the development of the apparatus of other companies as closely as it watched the Baird apparatus.

The principal firms to rival the Baird company in television were the Marconi company, HMV, and the Cossor concern. Marconi and HMV linked up with Electrical and Musical Industries Limited, EMI, soon to become John's most serious rival. By 1933 they had a mirror-drum system of mechanical television with two hundred and forty lines. This was about as far as the mechanical system could go, for there was a limit to the speed of the drum.

After this the rivals moved towards the electronic camera developed from Zworykin's iconoscope and to become the Emintro camera, a cathode-ray tube being used as a receiver.

To John it was obvious that he and the Baird company should join one or other of the larger companies or groups, so that resources and experience could be pooled. He said: "The Marconi company got in touch with us in 1932 and were anxious to join forces. We had numerous meetings, I went up to Chelmsford and was shown round their television research department. Many meetings and luncheons followed and the whole stage was set for a merger."

But John was reckoning without the board. He had never felt at ease with Ostrer who, with other members of the board, seemed to regard the company as an organization for selling television sets rather than as one for research. John's allies on the board were Captain A. D. G. West, who had joined the company in May 1933, and Sydney Moseley. Captain West, it will be remembered, had been one of the experts sent to Hastings by Odhams; then he had been chief research engineer in the BBC before going into the cinema world at Ealing. Ostrer had invited him to join the board, but as a technical expert he supported John. West, Moseley, and John were outvoted on the subject of a merger. As a result, Moseley resigned in June 1933.

The Marconi Company, appreciating the value of co-operation in tackling novel and difficult problems, linked up with EMI.

Then there was an attempt to merge with the General Electric Company Ltd, of which the chairman, Lord Hirst, was a friend of Major Church of the Baird company's board. Of the attempted merger with GEC John said: "The immense importance of such a tie-up was very obvious to me. Although we got as far as having regular technical meetings and our two research departments were working in unison, and although the GEC combine were anxious for an agreement, at the last minute Isidore Ostrer turned the whole thing down."

Major Church was most disappointed and remained on the board only out of friendship for John. It was thanks to Major Church that John received an honorary Fellowship of the Royal Society of Edinburgh.

During 1932 and 1933 John had been thinking seriously about turning to electronic methods. "By 1933," he said, "for outdoor scenes we used what is known as the intermediate film process, i.e. we photographed the scene to be transmitted with a cinematograph camera; rather an elaborate process of developing tanks enabled this film to be developed in a matter of seconds, and the film was then televised, a revolving perforated drum being used for scanning. This rather elaborate process was necessary as we could not get enough light directly to the scene itself. By using a film we could use the light from an arc light directly through the film on to the photo-electric cell. Later we experimented with a camera of the electronic type and had one of these installed in the BBC, but it was not sufficiently sensitive to compete with the iconoscope."

The consortium of Marconi, HMV, and EMI was concentrating on the electronic camera developed from Zworykin's iconoscope. They met many difficulties but to overcome them they had money, space, and a brilliant team of men.

The BBC was watching developments everywhere, bearing in mind that the contract with John ran no later than March 1934. It was not at all certain that the BBC would choose the Baird system when establishing a regular service on ultra-short waves; if the BBC rejected the Baird system, the Baird receivers would have become obsolete.

On 18 and 19 April engineers of the BBC saw and compared demonstrations of Baird and EMI television, with EMI making a favourable impression, though all that was shown was the transmission of films by television; definition was good and the method showed the promise of improvement.

The BBC avoided the responsibility of itself making the decision. In May 1934 the new Postmaster General, Sir Kingsley Wood, appointed a parliamentary committee to consider the matter. The chairman was Lord Selsdon, for that was the name which the former Postmaster General, Sir William Mitchell-Thomson, had taken on becoming a peer. What Sir Kingsley Wood required of the committee was that it should "consider the development of television" and "advise him on the relative merits of the several systems and on the conditions under which any public service should be provided."

The Selsdon committee was to issue its report in January 1935. Meanwhile John continued his experimental transmissions from the Crystal Palace, with an independent television service in mind.

Of the Selsdon report John said: "They were unable to choose between our apparatus and the apparatus of the Marconi-EMI. There was, I think, at the time, very little to choose between us. We had a system of two hundred and forty lines, the Marconi-EMI had adopted a four-hundred-line system of scanning developed by RCA and described in a patent taken out by Ballard, one of their assistants. They also used as transmitter an apparatus called an iconoscope, developed by the research department of RCA headed by Zworykin. As for actual results, we showed a better transmission of cinematograph film and close-ups, but our intermediate film was a clumsy and inefficient device compared with the iconoscope. The committee . . . recommended that both systems be tried by the BBC for a period of two years, after which the most satisfactory should be adopted."

It was not until August 1936 that the first high-definition show was launched by the BBC at Radio Olympia and not until 2 November that the two systems, Baird and Marconi-EMI, began to appear regularly week and week about, from the new BBC studio at Alexandra Palace.

While competition was changing the technical and financial background of television in England, Germany was undergoing rapid and radical change.

It was in February 1933 that John and I visited Germany together. It was very cold and soon John was ill. One of my many relations in Germany, a Dr Platau, an ear, throat, and nose specialist, attended John and told me sad stories of the difficulties put in the way of Jewish professional people, how they dreaded a knock at the door during the night, when one of the family, chosen at random, would be taken away to a concentration camp. Storm troopers stamped through the streets, swastikas hung from every window, and my relations in Berlin had good reason to be terrified.

John describes Germany and the company's time there: "The periodic visits I made to Germany in the early days were immensely happy. The dry, clean air of Berlin acted as a tonic and the comfort of the big German hotels far surpassed anything to be met with in London or America.

"When first I visited Berlin, like most English visitors, I went directly to the Adlon, being told it was the best hotel in Berlin. Major Church (a friend of Moseley's who had joined the board in 1931) pointed out that the Adlon was built and run for the express purpose of exploiting the tourist and that in fact the best hotel was the Kaiserhof. So there I transferred myself and it was there, before he came to power, that I saw Hitler for the first time.

"Major Church was a close friend of Chancellor Brüning, whom I met on many occasions. Brüning was a quiet, studious, impressive figure. I felt he was more of a scholar than a statesman. The last time I saw him was shortly after Hitler came to power when his life was in extreme danger.

"Church and I visited Brüning in a villa outside Berlin where he was staying with a friend. I remember the talk turning to the reformation of the race by sterilizing the unfit. The friend opposed it. 'It is too great a shock to the soul,' he said. Brüning nodded in agreement. I was struck by the use of the word 'soul' in a discussion of this kind, until I remembered Brüning was a devout Catholic.

"Hitler was the exact opposite of the dreaming, studious Brüning. He sat near me in the lounge of the Kaiserhof where every afternoon he took tea, surrounded by some dozen of his supporters. Göring and Goebbels were no doubt among them, but I did not recognize them: at that time they had not blazed into prominence.

"Hitler, however, could not pass unnoticed: he sat at the head of the table, his eyes staring in front of him with a strange, fixed look under a shock of black hair. He sat erect, silent and unmoving, except when some member of his party whispered respectfully to him and he would bow or shake his head.

"I gazed fascinated at the scene. The *maître d'hôtel* approached and warned me discreetly to look elsewhere. Nazis in brown shirts came to the table, gave the Nazi salute, took instructions, and departed briskly.

"I was told that it was a lot of nonsense and would soon fade away, that the man was a fanatic followed by a few out-of-works and others of no importance.

"My last visit to Berlin was in 1933 and I found Nazis everywhere. Nazi officials were on guard at every stall in the radio exhibition, swarms of them were in the streets, and hands everywhere were raised in the Nazi salute. 'Heil Hitler!' resounded on every side.

"Hitler was no longer to be seen in the Kaiserhof: he was in the chancellery. The Chancellor of Germany, Brüning, had fled for his life, the old régime had vanished, and a grim reign of terror had taken its place.

"The yearly visit to Berlin had been a delightful period among charming, happy, friendly people, hotels with every comfort, and smiling waiters anxious to please. This had vanished, no smile remained. The people had become grim and hostile, though not openly so. But it was obvious that those who were friendly and disliked the Nazi régime (there were many) were terrified.

"Hitler's coming to power had a further effect on our company.

"Fernseh A.G., which we originally formed in Germany and in which we had equal shares with Bosch, Zeiss, and Loewe, was leading German television. The Nazis were interested in the medium, and Church said that Goebbels had told him that it would be wonderful to show himself and Hitler in every German home!

"Hitler gave orders that our interest as a British concern must cease and that Fernseh must become wholly German. David Loewe, who had wanted us to take over the Loewe interest and gain control, had been expelled from Germany because he was a Jew.

"Fortunately Major Church was able to visit Germany and negotiate a deal whereby we got a substantial cash payment for our share. If Church had not acted promptly, Hitler would simply have confiscated the lot."

In January 1932, the month we left Box Hill and Isidore Ostrer took active control of the Baird company, I knew I was pregnant. John was elated for his dearest wish was for a child.

Nearly every week-end we escaped from London to Worthing; John loved the sea and we spent hours walking along the front.

Our daughter Diana was born on 5 September, a sweet and good baby, and I had an old-fashioned but kind nanny for her.

While I was still in the nursing home after Diana's birth John came in very upset, having learnt of his father's death. John and his father were alike in their tenacity, determination, and fierce independence. But as a father, John was never remote and Godlike in the manner of a Victorian father. As the children grew he played patiently with them and told them stories which he made up. His simplicity and directness of mind made him a perfect companion for children.

Our ideas of humour were not the same. For example,

soon after Diana was born, John had an appointment at Isidore Ostrer's house in Hamilton Place. On the way he stopped at Fortnum & Mason's and bought a haggis, to be a surprise for me. At Hamilton Place the butler took hat, coat, and haggis, and when John left he forgot the haggis. When he reached home he sadly told me what had happened, and I could hardly stop laughing. My laughter hurt him because he could see nothing funny in an absent-minded Scottish inventor leaving a haggis behind in the mansion of an illustrious Jew.

His own sense of humour could be coarse, cruel, and wounding. In 1934 I was in poor health and hoped to raise my spirits by having a new hat specially made, a hat with a brown felt crown and a brim of brown fluted velvet. When it arrived I put it on at once and turned to him for approval. He said: "You look like a whore!"

John was even rather proud of his command of bad language. As an apprentice he had worked among the lowest of what was then called the working class, with the fear of poverty and destitution never far away. In moments of stress he was liable to break into Saltmarket eloquence, in his rather high-flown words, "sufficient in its foul brutality and obscene imagery to cause a Billingsgate porter to stop his ears in horror."

What I found more depressing was his lack of enthusiasm for anything but television. He had no hobbies. He worked himself to a state of exhaustion and then recuperated in a state of complete inertia, lying in bed half the morning. Even then he kept in touch with his work through the telephone beside his bed.

Any kind of social life was impossible. One day a friend of my father's called and I had a happy afternoon hearing news of old friends. After he had gone I said to John: "Do you like him?" The reply was: "No. I thought he was a horrid man". My father's friend was a courteous and civilized gentleman.

That little incident was revealing. I think many Scots have an inferiority complex where England is concerned. Yet John's sympathies were not narrow. When we first met and I mentioned my Jewish ancestry, he said: "The Jews are the salt of the earth." But those with public school manners he distrusted on sight, perhaps because he had no confidence in his background, covering this lack by socialist sympathies and a coarse manner.

With friends, when he relaxed, he was the kindest and most charming of men. But he took an unreasoning and acute dislike to some people, and much of the unhappy relationship with the board stemmed from this.

It was in July 1933 that part of the Crystal Palace was rented. Then we settled down in our new house at 3 Crescent Wood Road, Sydenham. I knew nothing about a new house until John said one day that he had bought a house, adding: "I hope you will like it."

With Nanny and Diana I went by taxi to Sydenham, which I saw for the first time as a wilderness of broad and empty streets among large and decaying houses. Before 1914 Sydenham had been a fashionable suburb where the wealthy had built Gothic or Georgian houses for themselves, but fashion had long since passed Sydenham by.

The house which John had bought was Georgian, vast, with acres of bare floors and windows high out of reach. The old kitchen, with its pantry, maids' sitting-room, larder, and cellars, took my breath away. Weakly, I sat down on the steps. Nanny chose that moment to say: "Of course, madam, if you live here I'll have to give notice: all my friends are in Hampstead." Diana chose the next moment to cry.

There was nothing for it but to make 3 Crescent Wood Road habitable. The dining-room and the drawing-room opened into each other and measured sixty feet from end to end. The heating system required a man in the cellar all day, feeding coal into the furnace with a long-handled shovel. We never really warmed the house in winter.

John Logie Baird delivering a paper entitled 'Television – A General Survey' at the World Radio Convention

John Logie Baird demonstrating in 1939 the large cathode-ray tube which he named the Telechrome. The apparatus produced a three-dimensional picture in colour

I bought acres of Wilton carpeting and haunted auctions buying the largest pieces of furniture I could to fill the rooms. The final effect combined Jacobean and Chinese. We had a magnificent sideboard and table of dark oak, Chinese carpets and rugs, the decoration completed by the Chinese bowls and vases then fashionable.

The grounds covered three acres and contained four enormous beech trees, which John named Bach, Beethoven, Brahms, and Baird. He had the rose garden dug up and sweeping lawns laid out, probably because the garden of *The Lodge* at Helensburgh was mainly grass.

Before our marriage John had agreed that I should continue my career, but he was far from enthusiastic when I began to do so. In 1933 I started work again and fulfilled two engagements in Glasgow that March. John had not realized what a career as a concert pianist entailed and tried everything, even feigning illness, to prevent my going. Eventually he gave up but stipulated that I stay at the Central Station Hotel, the most expensive in Glasgow.

He became reconciled to my work, which must have sounded monotonous, though I tried to confine practising to times when he was out of the house. This outside interest was essential for me because our ordinary life was so strenuous. There were wires all over the house, on no account to be disturbed by cleaning, and relays of young technicians appeared at all hours of the day or night, all exhausted and all expecting innumerable cups of tea, which I had to provide. John worked them hard, though his usual courteous manner did something to disguise his impatience.

In the rest of 1933 I did several broadcasts and played at a number of concerts in Eastbourne, Bournemouth, and Harrogate with various orchestras.

John worked between his large, modern laboratory in the grounds of 3 Crescent Wood Road and the Crystal Palace. He never took me to a cinema and I took him to a symphony concert once only. Pouishnov was the soloist, and on going behind afterwards we were greeted like long-lost friends, Pouishnov more effusive than I had ever seen him.

XI. *The fighter*

So the two systems of television, the Baird and the Marconi-EMI, were to compete for two years, to ascertain which was the better, and the ceremony to open the competition took place at the Alexandra Palace on 2 November 1936. With notabilities of the BBC on the platform were Sir Harry Greer, chairman of the Baird company, who was televised by the Baird system and who said a few words, and Mr Alfred Clark, chairman of EMI, who was televised by the Marconi-EMI system and who also said a few words.

John, not invited to sit on the platform, remained in the body of the hall, furious at the slight by the BBC.

John knew that in the trial over two years he was in a difficult position. He was entirely dependent on a company controlled by Ostrer, a cinema magnate, and though he had loyal assistants, he alone was responsible for the work. EMI, on the other hand, had vast resources, the whole of the great RCA combine which, in addition to the largest companies in the United States, included the powerful Telefunken company in Germany and many others. As he put it: "If we had joined Marconi we should have been with this combine, not against it. Our policy of facing the world single-handed was sheer insanity: we should have made terms."

We were living in Crescent Wood Road and he was experimenting in his laboratory, attempting to improve the large screen, colour television, and stereoscopic television, his greatest success being with colour television.

John installed a big screen and projector in the Dominion Theatre in Tottenham Court Road and during 1936 showed colour television to audiences there. His screen measured twelve feet by nine, with a definition of a hundred and twenty lines. This was entirely mechanical and employed the Nipkow disc to scan the picture three times in three primary colours which were then superimposed. Several weeks were spent there showing black-and-white pictures too.

By the middle of 1937 meetings of the board had become intolerable and John, at his request, was given permission not to attend meetings.

Thereafter he worked in his laboratory in the grounds of 3 Crescent Wood Road; the garden was pleasant in the summer and we had afternoon tea out of doors or in the sun-room. John had been working on television for thirteen years and the strain was beginning to tell.

It must have been in 1934 that I looked out of an upstairs window and saw Diana, then about two, alone on the vast expanse of lawn and decided that she was not going to be an only child. John was against my going through it all again, but I talked him round and, on 2 July 1935, our son Malcolm was born.

I had no sleep for three months before the birth, a breech presentation, but Malcolm was healthy and energetic. For my recuperation my mother took me first to Tunbridge Wells and then to the South of France, where we stayed at my aunt's flat at Cagnes-sur-Mer.

My constitution showed none of the former resilience present after Diana's birth and it was a long time before I could return to normal life. While I was ill my sister-in-law, who had been on her own since her father died, came down to Sydenham.

A week after Malcolm was born John told me that the strain of my confinement had been so severe that he needed a holiday and was going to Morocco with Sydney. They also visited Tangiers, which he compared unfavourably with Australia, with its beautiful climate and scenery and "no filthy Arab beggars, as in North Africa, no indolent Negroes, as in the West Indies".

Then, on the Riviera, Sydney, speaking more French than John did, decoyed John into a barber's shop and told the man to cut John's hair really short. John was somewhat annoyed, only realizing what was happening when it was too late.

In fact I did not really recover from the effects of Malcolm's birth until we went to Australia as guests of the government in 1938, and by then the business had been transformed.

The trial of Baird and Marconi-EMI had not lasted anything like two years. It soon became obvious which of the two companies was the stronger, and John was further handicapped by a disastrous fire at the Crystal Palace.

Our house was less than a mile from the Crystal Palace. Late in the afternoon of 30 November 1936 the telephone rang and an hysterical voice told John that the Crystal Palace was burning down.

In his bedroom slippers John ran along the road to the Crystal Palace but before he reached Crystal Palace Parade he found the road blocked by motor-cars and a huge crowd. He elbowed his way to the front of the Crystal Palace, by then a mass of flames. The firemen were being hampered by the crowd, and before the fire was out the great main structure covered by glass, had been destroyed.

As that mass of glass melted the glow was seen over much of London; my mother and Diana, who was staying with her, watched the glow in the sky from the garden at Sutton, wondering what it was.

The old flooring-boards, which had been down for nearly a hundred years, must have been dry as tinder. Only a few offices under the south tower were saved, though the north tower survived.

With his ability to live strictly in the present John reported enjoying the spectacle as a spectacle, but the fire was disastrous for the company. He said: "In the fire we lost a hundred thousand pounds' worth of apparatus. True, a good deal of the value of this was recovered from the insurance, but the immense disorganization, loss of time, and loss of valuable records . . . occurred at the most awkward possible time and interfered seriously with our transmissions from the BBC.

Spare parts and apparatus which we were about to install were destroyed in the fire."

In spite of the fire the board was confident that the Baird system would be adopted by the BBC; Greer and Clayton, the only members who had Ostrer's ear, told him that everything was rosy and that Marconi-EMI had no chance. This was far from true, as John was aware, and he and his friends on the board, West and Church, could do nothing because Ostrer would not listen to them. More than ever John regretted Moseley's resignation.

Then the Postmaster General announced that the advisory committee on television had recommended that the dual transmissions come to an end, with the adoption of a single set of standards. The EMI system was chosen, and the BBC's last transmission of the Baird system was on 13 February 1937.

Of the decision John wrote: "And so, after all these years, we were out of the BBC. The fact that it was the RCA system, imported from America, the scanning used being covered by the RCA-Ballard patent and the transmitter being the iconoscope of Zworykin and the research department, did not hinder the Marconi company proclaiming the system all British. The iconoscope was now called the emitron. Ballard was ignored, and in an amazingly short time the Marconi publicity department had established it in the public mind that Marconi had invented television."

His own work was ignored, and to praise John would hardly have been in the interests of Marconi and EMI.

It seemed that he had been forgotten by the world. He bore up with practically no mention of his troubles to anyone and presented himself to his assistants and the press with his usual calm exterior, but I knew that inwardly he was seething. It is little wonder that he was bitter. I could not help him very much in his deep hurt and frustration. He was too deeply hurt for any superficial compensation.

He seemed to be tired and was often to be found resting on his bed.

The board was relieved by the turn which events had taken. Clayton, Ostrer's accountant, observed that the transmissions through the BBC had done nothing but lose money, the company's only hope of making money being the sale of receivers.

John was simply not interested in selling receivers.

The breach between his work as an experimenter and the board's salesmanship was virtually complete: he no longer attended meetings of the board and, from 1 January 1938, he resigned as managing director and became instead technical adviser to Baird Television Ltd. He withdrew to his private laboratory and there he concentrated on cinema television. His chief assistant was Paul Reveley, who had worked with him on the apparatus for the large screen in the Dominion Theatre, with the demonstrations there even before the BBC ended the transmissions.

Cinema television seemed to offer an opening for Baird Television Ltd as an independent entity and John lost no time in going into action.

Later he wrote: "It seemed to me that now, being out of the BBC, we should concentrate on television for the cinema and work hand-in-glove with Gaumont-British, installing screens in their cinemas and working towards the establishment of a broadcasting company independent of the BBC for the supply of television programmes to cinemas . . . I had built up a big screen and projector. This, with Isidore Ostrer's consent, had been installed in the Dominion Theatre, so that some sort of a start had been made. The BBC's decision was a blow to Ostrer, who was thoroughly dissatisfied and even hinting at withdrawing his support from the company, when, by a heaven-sent opportunity, I was thrown in contact with him at the television exhibition in the Science Museum.

"I was filled to exploding point with enthusiasm for cinema television and let him have it in full force. When once one had established contact, Ostrer was very impressionable and he rose at once.

"We had tea together and discussed the position at length.

" 'Some vital personality is needed to force this thing through', said Isidore Ostrer. 'We need fresh blood. It will be a big fight. We need a fighter'."

To John's delight the fighter chosen by Isidore Ostrer was Sydney A. Moseley.

With the promise of Moseley's return to the company John set to work with a will and gave Ostrer a demonstration on 4 February 1938; even the domestic staff at Crescent Wood Road shared in the champagne that followed. For his part, Ostrer brought Moseley into the offices at the Crystal Palace one day at the end of February. As the board had all but forced Moseley's resignation, some of the members were none too pleased to see him, but Ostrer's word was law. John's comment was that "they dissembled their grief and greeted him like a long-lost brother."

A new lease of life was one result of Moseley's return. It showed in an evening when Moseley and his wife, John and I took Diana to Southend; we went on all the roundabouts and shied at coconuts, finishing off with a drive along the front to see the illuminations. With Moseley present, John could relax and be his boisterous self again.

On the serious and business side a decision was taken to form a new company, Cinema Television Limited, which would virtually control Baird Television Limited. The only people to be in on this were Ostrer, John, West, and Moseley; and the new company was registered with a nominal capital of a quarter of a million pounds.

At the same time the Baird company was reorganized. John became president of the company at four thousand pounds a year. Greer remained chairman, and Clayton became managing director. Moseley was to come into the reorganized Baird company, but here trouble set in.

Moseley did not come in after all: members of the board were hostile to him and Ostrer decided that Moseley could be more useful off the board than on it. Moseley decided otherwise. In his book, *John Baird*, Moseley said: "Ostrer almost persuaded me to join the board in the first instance and I had another ally in Archie Church, but I did not see how I could work with some of the others, and, as I have said, I was too tired to start fighting all over again."

Moseley's second departure notwithstanding, Cinema Television looked a promising concern, and the company had one great advantage, a working system of television in colour that was good. The camera with its three colour filters was mounted on a truck and could produce excellent pictures on its cathode-ray monitor, taking natural scenes outdoors even on a cloudy day. Contrary to popular belief, John was fully aware of the advantages of cathode-ray tubes, and I remember our large hall at Sydenham littered with them as he unpacked them from their straw. In a letter to Thornton Bridgewater Paul Reveley said: "It is not true that Baird was indifferent to cathode-ray methods. Right from the start at Sydenham we used cathode-ray pictures as well as wave form monitors for our mechanically derived and received pictures . . .

"But he did not know enough about electronics to guide any purely electronic development of television effectively and he seems to have been unlucky with the choice of some early assistants who had not enough information and ability to translate ideas into practice.

"To my mind Baird's fundamental weakness was a chronic inability to see the need for detailed work before putting any project into action. Times without number he would ring up some supplier and say: 'Oh, Mr Lynes, we need a water-cooled box for a motor that is getting a little hot, say X by Y by Z inches. Could you make one for me, please?' Later on I had to make shift with whatever Mr Lynes, working from this vague specification, had thought would be suitable. It generally was not so, simply because all the implications had not been considered and worked out on paper first. For me, invention and paper-work are inextricably interrelated, the one feeding upon and cross-fertilizing the other.

"I believe, also, that he did not participate in any of the laboratory work because he could not do neat, professional-looking work with his hands. I do not think he was deterred by any feeling that it would have been undignified. He walked round once or twice a day to ask the inevitable question: 'Have you anything to show me, Mr Reveley?'

"The general directives of the work were always his; it was the detailed working out of means for accomplishment which he left to me. This was a good collaboration and a very happy time for me.

"I left Baird for the Colonial Engineering Service in November 1938 because I had come to realize that the resources he was deploying on the problems of television were not merely inadequate but by many orders too small to obtain success. I took this step with the greatest reluctance because he was the best boss as a person that anyone could hope to work for."

Early in 1938 the Australian government invited John to address the radio convention that was to be held in that country. He was reluctant to go during negotiations about cinema television, but I thought the change would do us both good; in any event he was eager to see Australia.

On 22 February we sailed from Marseilles in the *Strathaird*, and his invitation to me to accompany him had come in a truly Scots way: "If you come I shall have to pay your expenses, whereas if I take Sydney he will be paid for!"

I am glad I went with him, for that was the first time in our lives together that we were able to escape from the business worries of television. His cares diminished with every mile we travelled until he became like a young man.

He had not given me any details of what was to happen in Australia, and it was only when unpacking in the cabin in the

Strathaird that I found an itinerary crowded with functions, luncheons, and dinners in Perth, Adelaide, Melbourne, and Sydney, in fact wherever there was a branch of the Institute of Radio Engineers. I did not have appropriate clothes with me, but in Bombay I managed to buy some evening frocks at the Army and Navy Stores.

On arrival in Bombay telegrams greeted us from leading personalities in Indian radio, and on landing we found that the Maharajah of Kutch had invited us to be guests of honour at a dinner in the Taj Mahal Hotel on Malabar Hill.

Among the seventeen distinguished guests was the head of Indian Radio and Cable Telecommunications Ltd, S. T. Dockray. His Highness the Maharajah, an elderly man, was cultured and distinguished, and as the only woman present I was seated on his right hand. The elegance of the occasion, the frangipani on the table with its beautiful appointments, fairly took my breath away. This was the first time I had sat at table with any but white-skinned people. Fortunately I had been reading Rabindranath Tagore and was able to say so by way of conversation with the maharajah. "Ah yes," he said. "He was an intimate friend of mine." I could not help thinking that this race of people was civilized when the inhabitants of Britain were practically savages.

John, too, enjoyed that evening, but his constitution had not changed. He noted: "What a meal! All other banquets pale before it. Dish followed dish, each more delicious and exotic than the last. I ate heartily and was horribly ill for nearly a week afterwards. In fact we had reached Perth in Australia before my interior organs had got back to normal."

Smallpox broke out on board, and after vaccination and much talk we were allowed to land at Adelaide's outer harbour and take the train across Australia to Sydney, missing Melbourne and the arrangements there. In Perth, on the way, we were graciously met by Mr L. T. Bean, who represented our interests in Australia and had been responsible for arranging our visit. John spoke to the Perth Radio Society at a luncheon.

In Sydney we had a splendid reception. John's lecture, carefully prepared, was well received at Sydney University, as was his demonstration of a cathode-ray tube.

But what really impressed him were the two systems of broadcasting in Australia, the Australian Broadcasting Commission and the private stations with their advertising. About this he kept on saying: "This is what Britain needs." It is now what Britain has, BBC and ITV; but in those days the BBC maintained a strict monopoly.

John was against a monopoly of entertainment by any public body, believing that would lead to narrowness and conformity.

He enjoyed the visit to Australia, appreciating the absence of poverty-stricken natives, and he found the middle-class society a fulfilment of the socialistic dreams of his boyhood. He wrote: "In one of the many social Utopias of which I have heard it is proposed that no-one's income should exceed a thousand pounds a year. Beyond this figure income tax would be one hundred per cent. The establishment of an idle aristocracy would be prevented by one hundred per cent death duties, and with similar measures to prevent extreme poverty by state assistance the community would eliminate extremes of poverty and riches.

"In Australia this appeared to me to have been approximated to. I saw no acute poverty and no slums as we understand that term, and, on the other hand, I saw no evidence of flaunting wealth and found indeed an almost startling absence of anything in the nature of class distinctions. It was a country entirely inhabited by the petty bourgeoisie and as I myself belong to this class, I felt pleasantly at home."

That passage reminds us of change in Britain since 1938. Such ideas as John's are a commonplace in the welfare state, though a thousand pounds a year as the limit of an income has been rendered absurd by inflation.

But perhaps John and other individualistic men of his type would find it even more difficult to make their way in so highly organized a society.

On the way back from Australia, the nearer we got to London the more John's spirits fell. To London with its inevitable board meetings and difficulties was added the grave news from Germany.

But Cinema Television continued and big screens were installed at several more Gaumont cinemas, Baird Television Ltd produced and sold receivers, and the hope was that either or both would make a profit.

We returned to the house at Sydenham and on the surface life went on as before. For the children we had a charming young lady from Lincolnshire, Miss Yarker, as governess There were two country girls as maids.

I felt sure that there would be war and begun urging John to take us to South Africa. Moseley, too, read the signs correctly.

Eventually John took a furnished house for us at Minehead in Somerset, and although the imminence of war receded somewhat after Chamberlain's visit to Munich, we spent six months at Minehead. I passed the time there by organizing six concerts, one a month, and among others engaged Brosa, the violinist, Garda Hall, a South African singer, Betty Humby (who was to become Lady Beecham), and Gaby Valle, the soprano. I accompanied the soloists and enjoyed working again. At Christmas John came down loaded with parcels, stout for once and looking healthy.

We returned to Sydenham in January 1939 and in April we had three weeks at St Tropez.

The business was continuing in 1939 and even prospering. Ostrer announced that in all he would equip seventy cinemas in London with television screens, and many programmes already televised by the BBC were picked up by relay and shown at the cinemas which already had screens. Sales of receivers were good, there were about twenty-three thousand sets in the London area, and orders were pouring in for Baird home receivers. The sets cost about fifty guineas at that time, and Baird Television Ltd had a staff of nearly five hundred men.

In August 1939 the radio show opened at Radio Olympia, Baird Television with a first-class exhibit. Then the tension became impossible to bear and on 1 September the BBC's television service closed down and Radio Olympia came to an end.

XII. War and other irritations

It was at eleven on the morning of 3 September 1939 that Chamberlain announced that we were at war, and John and I then went to our room to discuss the situation. The telephone rang downstairs and when John came back from answering it he looked quite frantic. The directors of Gaumont-British had put the Baird company into the hands of the Receiver, so John's salary of four thousand pounds a year had stopped that day!

Then someone else telephoned, and this time the news was that the BBC had suspended all television transmissions for the duration of the war.

In two short hours our source of income had gone and with it all possibility of further developments of television for profit. John was president of a company that no longer existed.

The first thought was to get the children out of London because everyone expected that Hitler would use gas. John took a map and a ruler and drew a line westwards from London. The line ended at Bude on the Cornish coast, almost two hundred and fifty miles away. By persistence on the telephone at two o'clock in the morning he had us booked into a small hotel there. I hated leaving him, but there was no choice and, with suitcases packed in haste, we left the next day.

Bude was a quiet seaside resort, soon to be crammed with evacuees. There were already a number of families like ours there, but after a week or two I managed to find a furnished house. Miss Yarker had gone home, and as I did not have the house in Crescent Wood Road to run, I decided to look after the children myself. They loved country life and the broad beaches at Bude. I found a very good prep. school for them, one which had been evacuated from Bexhill.

Then John used his arts of persuasion on my mother and she left Sutton to join us. At the end of September she arrived at an hotel, having come by car for she had with her Sultan, a black labrador, Titus, a black cat, four canaries, and a pair of budgerigars. Later John brought down Smoky, a grey and white cat he had rescued from Sydenham. The animals were uneasy in the hotel and my mother joined us in our furnished house. She had been reluctant to leave Sutton and regretted the move more than we thought.

The staff of the Baird company dispersed into war service. John expected to be called on, but as in World War 1, but with less excuse, his country passed him over. This hurt him deeply.

He wrote: "When war was declared every order was cancelled as the BBC immediately stopped transmitting television programmes . . . Receivers became useless junk. Gaumont-British held some three hundred thousand pounds' worth of bonds in the company, the total capital of our company being one million and eighty thousand pounds. Shortly after war was declared, these bond-holders, under the terms of their bonds, installed receivers and ultimately put the company into liquidation, acquiring the company's assets in payment of their bonds. These assets were taken over by Cinema Television, owned and controlled by Gaumont-British. With my contract terminating with the appointment of the receivers, I became a free agent.

"I was in the middle of some extremely interesting and, I believed, important work on colour television, and rather than see this stopped I continued it at my own expense, keeping on two assistants and working in a private laboratory attached to my house at 3 Crescent Wood Road.

"I also sent in my name to the authorities and expected to be approached with some form of government work, but no such offer materialized. In the meantime colour television made very good progress and soon I was able to show a six-hundred-line colour picture of very fine quality. With

The house at No. 3 Crescent Wood Road, Sydenham, London S.E. 26, which the Bairds owned from 1932 to 1946

Leslie Mitchell of television fame and William Taynton (right), the first man to be seen on a television screen, in the public house called The John Baird near the Alexandra Palace, London
(Photograph by Herbert K. Nolan)

BAIRD'S 'FIRSTS'

1925 Baird demonstrated a silhouette transmitted by television
1926 Baird demonstrated live television of faces, using 30 lines
1926 Objects in total darkness televised by using infra-red rays
1927 Television from London to Glasgow by telephone line
1928 The first television picture made in normal daylight
1928 Photovision Video recording on wax discs
1928 Colour television achieved by scanning with spots of red, green, and blue light
1928 Three-dimensional television with the viewer observing the screen through a stereoscope
1929 Transmission from London on medium waves received at Bradford and on the Continent
1930 Simultaneous transmission of television and sound from Brookmans Park
1930 The first play televised in Baird's laboratory in Long Acre and transmitted by the BBC
1931 First public showing of a brilliant large screen, using a modulated arc lamp
1932 First television on ultra-short waves sent from Long Acre to Selfridge's
1933 The BBC takes over, televising on four nights a week, the picture on 261 m and sound on 399 m

the war raging . . . my only hope was to keep going until after the war."

In the laboratory, part of the old stable, he had a general handyman, Oxbrow, and a competent technician, Mr E. G. O. Anderson.

I visited London as often as I could, but it was impossible to keep the house at Sydenham going, and John lived in various hotels near by. Once more he was living uncomfortably in hotel bedrooms, but he felt the inconvenience of this kind of life far more now.

Bill, a local postman who used to do some gardening for us, continued to come round and helped to keep the place in some sort of order. But the windows were shattered twice by blast from bombs or guns, and all the gates and iron fences were taken to be melted down for armaments.

My journeys to London were so awful, in trains crowded after Dunkirk with shaken young troops evacuated from France and landed at Plymouth, that I learnt to go straight to the guard's van at Exeter and sit there on my suitcase eating sandwiches. If the weather was good I used to go to Sydenham and tried to clean it up, but in bad weather we stayed at the Palace Hotel in Bayswater.

I was usually too tired to care about raids, but John was curiously brave and we never took shelter except once, when the manager came to our room and ordered us downstairs. Otherwise, as the earth shuddered from an explosion near by, I used to ask: "Is that a bomb?" John used to reply: "No. Go to sleep. It's only the guns."

When I was in Cornwall John telephoned me every evening, trying to sound cheerful, but at Paddington station, where he used to meet me, my first glimpses of him showed his distress and dejection. The bombing must have been getting on his nerves and it was a distressing background to the continuous draining away of money. He was fast running through his fairly small savings, what with the establishment at Bude and the laboratory with two full-time assistants; he said it was like watching himself bleed to death. His only hope was to keep going somehow until television could be resumed.

In August Nipkow died in New York, his only recognition in eighty years of life an appointment in 1934, made for the sake of propaganda, as honorary president of the German Television Society.

Then followed for John a personal loss, the suicide of Mephy, whom he had just written to and arranged to visit. Ryde, opposite Portsmouth, had been having continual air-raid alarms. Mephy could not sleep and his nervous system must have given way. On the Friday morning he had his breakfast as usual, went to his studio in Herb Cottage, locked himself in, and gassed himself. When he did not return to his lodgings the police broke down the door and found him.

John rushed off to Ryde, arranged for the funeral, took over Mephy's personal effects, even retrieving some of his own letters kept for more than twenty years. All this upset him so much that he wired for me to join him and we spent a day or two resting at Salisbury.

Shortly after Mephy's death, depressed and in bad health, John took a drastic cure. He told me nothing and spent five or six weeks in a nursing home, Tempsford Hall in Bedfordshire, losing more than forty pounds. I was horrified when I met him at Exeter station. He was about half his usual girth, merely nibbled some biscuits instead of eating a meal, and was very pleased with himself. He said he felt much younger.

His account runs: "I had been in bad health for some time, and the continual air raids, which had blown out the windows of my house and brought down the ceiling of the room where I was boarding, were very upsetting. I decided to have a short holiday outside London and went to an hotel which also advertised medical treatment, with the intention of resting for a fortnight.

"When I arrived I had a heart attack and saw the resident

physician. He told me I was too fat, that fat was pressing on my heart and if I did not do something about it I was liable to drop dead at any moment. He undertook to cure me by a complete fast.

"Thoroughly frightened by his diagnosis I went through the treatment, rigorous though it was, and fasted for fifty days. For the first two weeks I had a few ounces daily of raw carrot and mustard-and-cress, but this brought on acute sickness and had to be stopped. For a fortnight I lived on nothing but water, and for the rest of the time I was allowed twelve grapes daily. At the end of the time . . ., whatever my appearance, I certainly felt better.

"I used to wander about in the grounds of the hotel and made many pleasant friends, among them Philip Morrell . . . He forcibly suggested that I should write my autobiography before the details faded from my mind . . ., so during the cure . . . I asked a typist to call at the hotel, and it was there that the first chapter of *Sermons, Socks, and Television* was dictated."

It is here that his notes for an autobiography come to an end. He worked on them up to the last months of his life, but as they are merely a first draft they cannot be published as they stand. Moseley has used some vivid passages in his *John Baird*, and I have tried to select the best parts for this book.

It was not only colour television which occupied John's attention during the war, and he spent much time in an attempt to help with the war by inventing a new method of transmitting printed matter by television, his aim being the transmission of half a million words a minute. This he called facsimile television.

All records of the invention seem to have disappeared, but there is an account in *The Manchester Guardian*, as it was then called, of 17 August 1944.

"Mr John Baird, inventor of television, is planning to

revolutionize wireless telegraphy so that complete typewritten pages may be sent at the rate of twenty-five a second to anywhere in the world. The present speed, used largely for pictures, is one page every six to ten minutes.

"Today messages written in London to be wirelessed overseas have to be changed letter by letter and word by word into electrical impulses which are broadcast and then translated into letters and words again at the receiving end. Mr. Baird intends to increase the speed of photo-telegraphy, sending pictures by wireless, by some fifteen thousand times, and he proposes to radio not only pictures but plans and messages. Blueprints, charts, machine and architectural drawings, and newspapers could, he says, be radioed in seconds.

"At the moment Mr. Baird is working on the elimination of the only serious difficulty: the new system will have to be operated on ultra-short waves and will travel only comparatively short distances before the message or picture fades. By having equipment to pick up and relay the impulses every fifty miles of the route, messages and pictures could be sent at twenty-five a second from, say, London to Rome.

"At the moment there is no means of transatlantic transmission. Mr Baird is convinced that these difficulties will be overcome. He said yesterday that his new instrument makes an international newspaper possible. A whole newspaper could be transmitted about the world in a matter of seconds."

That was in 1944. In 1946 John died but others developed the idea, and Mr Anderson, who joined John in 1938 and was his chief assistant during the war, has written: "Ultrafex and the telerecording system, which has been so useful, were based on the telefilm recording technique."

That was a diversion to which I shall return when I introduce Sir Edward Wilshaw.

Meanwhile, on 23 October 1940, John took out a patent for colour television with six hundred lines; he showed it to the press on 14 January 1941, but news of war was more important than news of inventions.

With Moseley in the United States, working at British propaganda and trying to persuade John to join him, there were possibilities, opportunities for research in the United States, but John would have to be on the spot to seize them. John was tired and preferred to remain in his laboratory and sit out the war.

About this time John visited Hutchinson, married and prosperous on a small farm outside Brighton. John wrote jokingly to Moseley that they might start another Television Ltd., and sent him full particulars of his superscreen tele-radiogram in the hope that some American would be impressed. It was far ahead of its time.

Then the financial situation was saved once more, this time by Sir Edward Wilshaw, who was chairman of Cable and Wireless and had for a long time been an admirer of John's work. In 1941 Sir Edward engaged John as consultant technical adviser to his firm, the appointment being without conditions but with remuneration at the rate of a thousand pounds a year. This left John free to carry on with his research, while the money was enough to pay for the laboratory and part of the salaries of the assistants.

Sir Edward's gesture, besides saving the financial situation, did much to restore John's self-respect, sadly damaged by the government's neglect to make use of him in wartime. He was very grateful to Cable and Wireless (since nationalized) and when well enough attended their office once a fortnight.

If he had lived he might have perfected facsimile television for them. Sir Edward, in a letter dated 7 August 1951 and quoted by Moseley in his book, said: "I had no doubt, and I still have no doubt, that the ultimate end of telegraphy will be some form of picture transmission of the written word rather than the mechanical process of the punched slip."

Slowly, as the children grew in the healthy air at Bude, John had become a family man. When Diana was born he tended to regard her as another experiment, but he gradually became aware that she and Malcolm would very likely be with us for a long time!

Whenever he came to Bude he would sit in the garden and quote to the children from *Alice in Wonderland* and Edward Lear. He began the story of a pair of flies, Izzy and Dizzy, who lived with their mother, Mrs Flossy Flannelfeet, in various hotels and suffered from the cold and wartime food, thus transferring his own trials to the flies.

He tried to interest the children in optics, buying them poster paints and showing them how to mix the primary colours to obtain various shades. And when we were living on the farm – for during 1943 we rented half a farmhouse – he bought Diana a magnifying glass and they set fire to newspapers by concentrating the sun's rays. He taught the children to make telephones, first with Klim tins and string and later by a more elaborate system which used batteries.

These experiments were rather wasted on Diana, but Malcolm understood them and they might have started him off on his own scientific career.

What Diana enjoyed was walking with her father, and together they explored the cliffs and the network of lanes which link Bude and Stratton. He walked very slowly, which suited a child, and like a child he was able to live in the present and enjoy looking at the plants and the animals they passed. When it came to the sea he would turn up the bottoms of his trouserlegs and walk for miles where sea met beach: the salt was good for his feet and the sight of the long lines of surf relaxed his mind.

At Bude he looked the part of inventor, with long hair, cloth cap pulled well down for warmth and also a symbol of his socialist principles, and a black overcoat with an astrakhan collar. One day, sitting on the beach, particularly dishevelled and making notes about television in a notebook, he was approached by a youth in uniform. I thought the youth was asking for an autograph, but the conversation lasted so long that I went and joined them. John, scarlet in the face with anger, was trying to convince the youth that he was not a spy! He had no papers on him, and it took me quite a few minutes and the production of John's ration book to convince the young military policeman that this was John Logie Baird, president of the non-existent Baird Television Company. The military policeman had never heard of Baird or television, but after a lot more talk he let us go home.

John's visits to Bude were a relaxation and he formed a circle of admiring friends among the people spending their retirement at Bude, but what he considered a waste of time made him fret.

He would then rush back to London, uncomfortable as it was with sirens, air raids, restrictions, and disruption. He visited old friends and found them all absorbed in their war work or that of their children. Jack Buchanan kept various theatrical shows running almost throughout the war and confided to us that the strain was terrible.

Meanwhile, between doing chores, I practised. In November 1942 I played the Mozart A Major Concerto (K 488) with an orchestra in the pavilion at Torquay. Noel Edie, a good Scottish singer, was among some notable musicians at Bude, and I accompanied her at concerts for the Red Cross. These concerts were organized by Dr D. G. A. Fox, a fine musician and organist, with one arm, director of music at Clifton College, evacuated southwards from Bristol.

In 1943 John sat for Donald Gilbert, the sculptor, who cast a bronze bust which John could not afford to buy. A copy is in the Hermitage Park at Helensburgh and the original in the National Portrait Gallery. The most vivid likeness is the painting by Keir-Lawson, showing the determined chin and the kindness in his gaze.

It was in this year, 1943, that the British government showed that it was not quite unaware of John and his work.

XIII. *Keeping right on*

In 1943 the government called up Mr Anderson, John's chief assistant, and this was a disaster as the work he did in the laboratory was vital. John, determined to keep Mr Anderson, went before the tribunal, with me accompanying him, in a desperate attempt to get an exemption. We failed, but John appealed and the appeal was upheld, Mr Anderson staying with John until the end.

But individuals associated with government had John in mind and in January 1944 the Hankey Committee was formed to consider the future of television when the war was over. There were doubts whether television should start again where it had left off, with a definition of four hundred and five lines and ultra-short waves, whether the government and the BBC should wait for a better system to evolve.

On 18 January Mr Attlee rose in the House of Commons and named the committee, of which Lord Hankey was chairman. Sir Noel Ashbridge and Mr Robert Foot represented the BBC, Sir Raymond Birch and Sir Stanley Angwin represented the Post Office, Mr Harvey represented the Treasury, for funds were likely to be the usual stumbling block, and two experts from the world of science and engineering were Sir Edward Appleton and Professor Cockcroft.

The committee decided to ask John's advice, and in March 1944 John had a letter from Lord Hankey at the office of the Privy Council. The letter took the form of a series of questions under six headings, and in his reply John observed that he spoke as a private individual carrying on research in his own laboratory.

In replying to the question about reopening the television service on the standard of 1939 John suggested that the service be started again as soon as possible, using the old standard of four hundred and five lines, provided that after three years a new system would render existing sets obsolete. The public and the trade should be warned well in advance of such obsolescence.

The next two questions were about research and the form which an improved service might take. John said that owing to limitations in the range of transmissions, relay stations should be used. There were no artificial satellites then, though by 1945 Arthur C. Clarke, a British electronics engineer, published his theory in *Wireless World* that artificial satellites could relay television to the whole of the earth. John suggested that a new service could be extended to the Continent and America, consisting of a thousand lines of stereoscopic television in colour.

The last two questions were about markets, domestic and overseas. John put forward his favourite theory of free competition for the domestic market, the abolition of the BBC's monopoly, and local services for Scotland and other regions, all of which are a reality now. Considering the market overseas, he made the interesting observation that Russia could be the largest potential market. That was before the Iron Curtain was lowered. To encourage exports, he suggested an international standard of television communication, not yet a reality.

On 28 March 1945 the Hankey report appeared as a White Paper. It recommended that television be resumed on four hundred and five lines as soon as possible after the war, though definition should eventually be a thousand lines, as John had recommended. Television should be extended from London to the six next most populous centres; it should be under the minister responsible for broadcasting sound and operated by the BBC. An advisory committee, including representatives of the Treasury, the Post Office, and the Department of Scientific and Industrial Research, should keep the scope of extension under constant review.

The report stressed the influence of domestic developments upon export and urged that vigorous research, under government control, should take place when staff became available, the aim being a standard of definition approaching that of the cinema, possibly incorporating colour and stereoscopic effects. Parliament accepted the report on 9 October 1945, and the BBC announced that as soon as possible it would resume television services from Alexandra Palace.

The main fact emerging from the report was the importance and complexity of television's organization. From a gadget in an attic, a toy for wireless fans, it had become a great industry needing careful handling by a government if it was not to have a harmful influence upon society.

Meanwhile John had perfected his last and perhaps greatest invention, the telechrome, an all-electronic system of colour television. On 16 August 1944 he demonstrated it and facsimile television. Next day *The News Chronicle* reported:

"By means of a new cathode-ray tube Mr Baird has caused a new medium of perfect colour to blend with his stereoscopic television. As I stood by the camera I saw my own photograph flash on to the television screen across the room. The image was in colour as natural as any colour film I have seen. The light wood grain of my pipe stood out clearly, a bead of perspiration on my forehead was highlighted, and the book in my hand was pictured so plainly that the coloured title of it could be read. I moved my hand backwards and forwards, tilted a cigarette packet away from the camera and saw the effect of distance on the screen was quite natural . . .

"Mr Baird smiled at the suggestion that the government might be induced to help him in his work and find him a laboratory in a safe area. 'That would be very nice,' he agreed, 'but I doubt if the government is interested enough to do any such thing. I have been given no tangible evidence of government interest,' he added. 'There is no doubt at all that after the war television will become an important industry and I feel that with these two inventions we have the opportunity of going ahead with the work'."

The war was coming to an end. John's health was failing. Soon the journey of eight hours to Bude was too much for him, and early in 1945 I went to Bexhill to find a house. We picked Bexhill because the children's school, Sandown, was returning there and also because John wanted to live at the coast but near enough to London to control a new company he was forming.

I found an unfurnished house to rent and moved an ailing mother, two children, the inevitable birds and animals, furniture from Sutton and Sydenham, and all the things we had accumulated at Bude. John was so breathless that he could not lift a suitcase, and my mother, with heart trouble, was a virtual invalid.

Bexhill, exposed to the east winds, was cold; I knew no-one except the teachers at Sandown, and John and my mother were invalids. I did much of John's correspondence for him.

He was very ill but determined to carry on. Jack Buchanan put up a sum of money and they floated a new company to develop cinema television in colour. This called for new premises in London with John travelling from Bexhill to London and back.

One day in February 1946 he went for a walk, came back tired, went to bed, and had a stroke during the night. We had nurses for him as my own health was at breaking point. My mother was almost bedridden, and the district nurse used to come in once a week to help her with her bath.

John was restless and ill; supposed to stay in bed, he used to get up and wander around the house. He had a longing for fruit, hard to find so soon after the war, and we sent to Covent Garden for grapes. In every room we had a coal fire and an electric heater, in spite of which John was always cold, sleeping at night with his electric blanket full on. Our bill for electricity ran at about sixty-five pounds a quarter, which alarmed me. He dreamed of a holiday in the sun, even talked of visiting South Africa, but a dream was all it was.

As summer came he was able to go for short walks. I was glad and said: "You are much better than you were."

He looked at me and said: "I am much worse."

On 14 June he was having a restless night. I gave him a drink of water and he looked at me and said: "In spite of all thy faults I love thee still."

We settled down and I waited to hear him breathing quietly before I went off to sleep.

When I woke next morning the room was unnaturally quiet and I knew at first glance that he was dead.

John's death followed by a week the restoration of television services by the BBC, one of whose first tasks was to televise the Victory Parade. But, with John, died cinema television, for without his drive the new company collapsed and the owners of cinemas, coming to the conclusion that television in the home was a threat to their very existence, decided not to have the equipment for television in cinemas.

But what cinema television promised is reflected in an extract from *Today's Cinema* of 11 June 1946:

"Marking the reopening of the BBC television service on Friday with the Victory Parade, a test demonstration was given of the latest Mark 11 big-screen projected television equipment manufactured by John Logie Baird Ltd. This demonstration took place at the Classic Cinema, Baker Street. Other equipment was installed in the New Theatre, Agar Street, and in the Savoy Hotel . . . With a throw of some fifteen to twenty feet a picture approximately fourteen feet can be secured."

John died as he had lived, undefeated. He was tired and it may be as well that he was spared the struggle of founding a company and the austerities after the war. He had never spared himself in his work, making no allowances for poor health, lack of money, and domestic upheavals. I knew him better than anyone else did and perhaps saw more than others his moods of depression when he would lie in bed all day long brooding over some reverse. Those fits of depression did not last long and the rebound from them was one full of enthusiasm and vitality. He lived in the present and gave the force of his powerful personality to what he was doing: work, horseplay with Moseley, or relaxed discussion with his friends.

Life with him was an exciting experience and I still find myself assuming the attitude he would have taken towards a particular situation: I can hear the remark he would have made with his unique sense of humour. My life and the lives of his immediate associates were never dull, due to his habit of taking action first and then presenting us with an accomplished fact. My rebellious and impatient temperament underwent a training which corrected many of my worst faults.

He is remembered for his power of concentration and his hatred of violence, but what I remember best is his courage.

Immediately after his death I decided that so great a man should be buried at his birthplace, arranging for the funeral to be in Scotland and his body to be buried beside his parents in the cemetery at Helensburgh. Friends and assistants went to Scotland for the funeral.

When John died Jack Buchanan sold the assets of the new company they had formed. Parts of the assets changed hands time and again, and by the early 1950s the trade-name Baird had become the property of Mr A. W. M. Hartley, with a company known as Baird-Hartley Ltd. Mr Hartley, to whom I am grateful, arranged a modest annuity for me, at the suggestion of Mr Seeman, a director.

It was in 1956, I think, that I was invited to the Rudolph Steiner Hall in London where a rather poor play, *The Life of John Baird*, was being broadcast through Radio Luxemburg. This was done in a spirit of admiration and I began to see that he had not been forgotten.

That year, too, the independent television companies came

into being, amid jubilation and enthusiasm, John's dream of a monopoly broken coming true.

Leslie Mitchell, charming and gallant, came out to Harrow and took me to a studio where we made a short and informal film for the opening programme of the first transmission of independent television. I said a few words about how grateful John would have been and how glad I was that so many more people would in consequence be employed in television, with independence making the industry as a whole expand.

Towards the end of 1957 the BBC asked me to supply all the information I had for their programme "This is your life", breaking all precedents by producing a posthumous account. Eamonn Andrews introduced all the characters, among them William Taynton, the first man to be televised, and Sydney Moseley. The cameras were brought right up to me at the climax, where I sat in a front stall, and Eamonn Andrews presented me with the scenario of "This is your life, John Logie Baird", in the form of a book.

In 1958 Malcolm and I went to South Africa, he for the two months of his university vacation, I for eight months. Just before we left, Rhona Churchill wrote about us in *The Daily Mail*, and her article produced a response from Norman Collins of ITV. He started a memorial fund for me and my family, drawing generous contributions from many of the leading companies manufacturing television sets in Britain, the total reaching nearly four thousand pounds.

Arrangements were then being made for the first Baird lecture at what was then called the Glasgow Royal College of Science and Technology, for which I went to Scotland on 17 March 1959. Thornton H. Bridgewater, M.I.E.E., delivered the lecture, *Baird and Television*, using much equipment from the BBC to illustrate what he said. The lecture is now delivered every other year, and the fund also provides a medal and a prize for students of electrical engineering in their final year at this university. By the time of the first lecture Malcolm was at Cambridge, working for a doctorate in chemical engineering. My daughter Diana, who has a master's degree in English, had married Norman Richardson in 1958 and was living in Scotland.

At the end of 1959 I returned to South Africa and made my home in Cape Town. There I recorded a long talk about John and television for the archives of the South African Broadcasting Corporation.

But popular fame may lie in other directions and that year a public house near the Alexandra Palace, owned by Courage & Barclay Ltd, was named The John Baird. Malcolm and many celebrities of television and the BBC attended the opening ceremony.

In 1960 the A.B.C. Independent Television learnt that I wanted to see Malcolm before he left for Canada and cabled me that they would pay my fare both ways.

Back again in South Africa I had letters from Mr A. W. M. Hartley and Mr P. Perring-Thoms to say that Mr Hartley had sold the trade-name Baird to Mr Perring-Thoms's vast Radio Rentals group, which had decided to manufacture television sets. It appeared that when the directors were discussing a name for this subsidiary company someone said, rather facetiously: "What we want is a name like Baird." Mr Perring-Thoms traced the name to the possession of Mr Hartley and bought it.

I am also as grateful to the late Mr Perring-Thoms as I am to Mr Hartley. Mr Perring-Thoms obtained from me a mass of information about John, his friends, and his associates. He found these people, and when I went to England in 1961 to meet the chairman of the new Baird Television Company, with his wife, the directors, and the staff, I found that he had arranged a series of happy meetings, press shows, luncheons, and dinners. On 31 May 1961 a dinner and reception for me were held at the Dorchester.

On 13 June I was taken to Bradford to see the new Baird factory, then with nearly a thousand employees.

The next year I made a concert tour of South Africa, playing in twenty-nine towns.

I went to Britain in 1963, primarily for the birth of a grandchild and to welcome Malcolm back from Canada. He has since left Edinburgh University for Canada again, where he is a professor of chemical engineering at McMaster University, Hamilton, Ontario. He is married and has two sons.

When I arrived in Britain that year I was taken to an enormous press conference at the Savoy arranged by Radio Rentals, with Mr and Mrs Perring-Thoms to welcome me. A model of the earliest Baird receiver stood next to the latest sets.

Twelve days later, on 26 August, at a dinner at the Savoy arranged by Radio Rentals, I presented the first television travelling scholarships awarded by the Television Society.

The following year, when I was back in Cape Town, Radio Rentals cabled me and asked me to fly to London and present commemorative silver Baird medallions to thirty leading personalities in television. This was at a gala function in the Albert Hall on 16 April.

I was saddened by the news of Mr Perring-Thoms's death, which occurred on 31 July that year. Fortunately the resulting changes which his death brought about did not mean the disappearance of the name Baird from the world of television, for Sir Jules Thorne of Thorne Electrical Industries acquired ownership of the trade-name and continues to manufacture Baird television sets.

Sir Jules had been kind enough to continue my annuity, at the same time recognizing the reality of inflation and twice increasing the annuity.

Other friends who have died include Geoffrey Parr of the Television Society, the sculptor Donald Gilbert, and Sydney Moseley, each having helped to perpetuate the name of John Logie Baird.

Perpetuated it should be for, besides being a great man of vision, a patient, humble, and courageous man, he was a man who forged ahead where many another would have stumbled and fallen.